D0126154

Contents

Introduction

This Pocket Dictionary is an indispensable companion for visitors to Korea and for anyone in the early stages of learning Korean. It contains all the 3,000 or so Korean words that are most commonly encountered in colloquial, everyday speech.

For the sake of clarity, only the common Korean equivalents for each English word have been given. When an English word has more than one possible meaning, with different Korean equivalents, each meaning is listed separately, with a clear explanatory gloss. The layout is clear and accessible, with none of the abbreviations and dense nests of entries typical of many small dictionaries.

Korean is spoken in both South Korea (the Republic of Korea) and North Korea (the Democratic People's Republic of Korea), as well as in parts of China, Japan, and Central Asian nations such as Kazakhstan and Uzbekistan (formerly republics of the Soviet Union), and has well over 70 million speakers in the Korean peninsula alone.

It is not clearly related to any other languages of the world, although some linguists claim that it belongs to the Altaic family, which is made up of the Turkic, Mongolian, and Manchu language groups. It also has some striking structural similarities to Japanese, but whether Korean and Japanese are genetically related remains in dispute.

The earliest form of the Korean writing system, dating from the early centuries CE and known as *Idu*, was also borrowed from Chinese, but was not widely adopted because of the structural and phonetic differences between the languages. From many centuries, Chinese was accepted as the literary language of Korea, and the native vernacular was not recorded in writing.

The current form of written Korean (known as Hangeul in South Korea and as Joseongeul in North Korea) was invented in the 15th century at the command of King Sejong. However, for some centuries thereafter it was eschewed by the literate in favor of expression in Chinese; only toward the end of the 19th century was literacy in Korean promoted as an instrument of national pride.

In Korean script each syllable is represented by a cluster of elements representing the constituent consonants and vowels, normally arranged from left to right and top to bottom within the cluster. In South Korea there is also still some limited use of

Chinese characters mixed in with Hangeul, although these differ somewhat from the forms now used in China, and their pronunciation has been adapted to Korean.

In this dictionary every Korean word and phrase is written in the Korean script, and also clearly transliterated into the roman alphabet. There is no universally agreed way of writing Korean in the roman alphabet, but this dictionary uses the new system approved and implemented by the South Korean government in 2000. The Korean-English section of the dictionary is arranged according to the alphabetical order of these romanized forms.

For guidance on the pronunciation, please see the separate section following. Korean is not a tonal language, but it does have an unfamiliar set of 'tensed' consonants, represented in this transcription by double letters.

The Korean verbs are given in the traditional 'dictionary form', unmarked for the differences in speech style between 'informal polite', 'formal polite' and 'plain'.

Pronunciation

Korean words and expressions in this book are romanized using the Revised Romanization of Korean prepared and authorized by the Korean Government (see below). Along with the principles of this system, some transcription conventions are adopted as follows:

(a) Words are romanized according to sound rather than to Korean spelling. However, in the case of verbs, the transcription of tensed sounds has been minimized so that the user can identify and utilize the verb stem without much confusion (e.g. to be = *itda*, instead of *itta*).

(b) Where there is an expression consisting of more than one word, a space is given to mark the word boundary.

(c) Where necessary, a dot (.) is used to mark the syllable boundary so that confusion in pronunciation can be avoided.

(d) Three dots (...) are used in a grammatical phrase where a noun is required.

(e) A hyphen (-) is used to indicate a verb stem or the optional adjective form derived from an adjectival verb.

(f) For descriptive words, both adjectival verb forms (e.g. to be pretty = *yeppeuda*) and adjective forms (e.g. pretty = *yeppeun*) are given.

The Korean alphabet and its romanization (revised in 2000)

1) Consonants

   (a) Simple consonants

ㄱ g, k	ㄴ n	ㄷ d, t	ㄹ r, l	ㅁ m
ㅂ b, p	ㅅ s	ㅇ ng	ㅈ j	ㅊ ch
ㅋ k	ㅌ t	ㅍ p	ㅎ h	

   (b) Double consonants

ㄲ kk	ㄸ tt	ㅃ pp	ㅆ ss	ㅉ jj

2) Vowels

   (a) Simple vowels

ㅏ a	ㅓ eo	ㅗ o	ㅜ u	ㅡ eu
ㅣ i	ㅐ ae	ㅔ e	ㅚ oe	ㅟ wi

   (b) Compound vowels

ㅑ ya	ㅕ yeo	ㅛ yo	ㅠ yu	ㅒ yae
ㅖ ye	ㅘ wa	ㅙ wae	ㅝ wo	ㅞ we
ㅢ ui				

Reading romanized Korean

There is a very important distinction between the reading of romanized Korean and English. The Korean romanization system depicts the sound of Korean in English letters to help foreigners communicate in Korean. Because English letters used in romanized Korean are sound symbols, they have to be pronounced in a certain way only. They should not be treated as those in English words. In English words, the sound value assigned to a certain letter varies according to different words. For example, 'a' in *apple, father, syllable* and *date* all have different sound values. Unless you have learnt the English phonetic symbols, you might read romanized Korean 'a' differently from the expected sound depending on what romanized Korean words you have. For example, you might read a as 'a' in *apple* when you get the romanized Korean word *sam* [삼] 'three'; or you might read it as 'a' in *syllable* for either *a* in the romanized Korean word *saram* [사람] 'person', etc.

To avoid this type of confusion, some examples of English words containing sounds equivalent to some of the romanized Korean vowels and consonants are given below (approximate guideline only):

Vowels: *eo, eu, ae* and *oe* are single vowels in romanized Korean as shown below. Therefore careful attention should be given to these vowels in not splitting them into two. Also, careful attention should be given to *u* [우] not to be read as English 'you'. Some common vowels which might confuse you are:

a	아	**ah**, f**a**ther	(but shorter)
eo	어	b**ir**d, s**e**rve	
o	오	b**a**ll, p**o**re	(but shorter)
u	우	sh**oe**, sch**oo**l	(but shorter)
eu	으	br**o**ken, g**o**lden	
i	이	b**ee**, sh**ee**p	(but shorter)
ae	애	**a**pple, b**a**d	
e	에	b**e**d, **e**gg	
oe	외	w**e**t, w**e**lcome	

Consonants: There won't be much trouble in pronouncing romanized Korean consonants except some tensed ones which require a relatively strong muscular effort in the vocal organs without the expulsion of air. Some examples are given as follow:

kk	ㄲ	s**k**i, s**k**y	(k after s)
tt	ㄸ	s**t**eak, s**t**ing	(t after s)
pp	ㅃ	s**p**eak, s**p**y	(p after s)
ss	ㅆ	**s**ea, **s**ir	(s before a vowel)
jj	ㅉ	bri**dg**e, mi**dg**et	(similar to a tutting sound in an exhaling way)

Korean–English

A

-a/eo boda -아/어 보다 try out -ing

-a/eo deurida -아/어 드리다 (humble form of -어/아 주다)

-a/eo juda -아/어 주다 do something for another's benefit

-a/eo juseyo -아/어 주세요 please (request for something)

-a/eodo jota -아/어도 좋다 may, can, be allowed to

-a/eoya hada -아/어야 하다 must, have to, ought to

abeoji 아버지 father

achim 아침 morning

achim iljjik 아침 일찍 early in the morning

achim siksa 아침 식사 breakfast, morning meal

achim siksahada 아침 식사 하다 breakfast, to eat

adeul 아들 son

(ae)hobak (애)호박 zucchini, courgettes

aejeong 애정 affection

aekjeot 액젓 fish sauce

aewandongmul 애완동물 pet animal

agassi 아가씨 you (young female adult)

agi 아기 baby

aheun 아흔 ninety

ahop 아홉 nine

ai 아이 child, offspring

aillaendeu 아일랜드 Ireland

aiseu keurim 아이스 크림 ice cream

ajeossi 아저씨 uncle, you (male adult)

ajik 아직 still, even now

ajik 아직 yet: not yet

aju 아주 very, so, pretty, quite, extremely

aju keuda/keun 아주 크다/ 큰 grand, great

ajumeoni 아주머니 aunt, you (married female)

al 알 egg

alda 알다 acquainted, to be

alda 알다 know, to

allak uija 안락 의자 armchair

allida 알리다 inform, let someone know, to

allyak 알약 pills, tablets

ama 아마 perhaps, maybe, possibly, probably

amho 암호 password

amnyeok 압력 pressure

amso 암소 cow

amudo -ji anta 아무도 -지 않다 nobody

amudo ...anida 아무도 ...아니다 nobody

amugeotdo anim 아무것도 아님 nothing

an 안 no, not (with verbs and adjectives), don't

anieyo 아니예요 no answer you're welcome

an ikda/igeun 안 익다/익은 unripe

an.gae 안개 fog, mist

an.gyeong 안경 glasses, eyeglasses, spectacles

anae 아내 wife

anbujeonhada 안부전하다 say hello, to

an(j)da 앉다 sit down, to

andwaetda! 안 됐다! pity: what a pity!

A

...ane(seo) ...안에(서) inside of

aneun saram 아는 사람 acquaintance

...aneuro ...안으로 into

...anida ...아니다 no, not (with nouns)

anio 아니오 no (answer)

anjeonhada, anjeonhan 안전하다, 안전한 secure, safe

anjjok 안쪽 inside

annaehada 안내하다 lead (to guide someone to somewhere)

annaeseo 안내서 guidebook

annaeso 안내소 information booth

annyeonghaseyo 안녕하세요 hello, hi, how are you?

annyeonghi gaseyo 안녕히 가세요 goodbye to a person leaving

annyeonghi gyeseyo 안녕히 계세요 goodbye to a person staying

apateu 아파트 apartment, flat

...ape(seo) ...앞에(서) before, in front of

apeuda 아프다 ache, to

apeuda, apeun 아프다, 아픈 ill, sick, sore, painful

apeuge hada 아프게 하다 hurt (cause pain), to

apeuro 앞으로 forward

apeuro naagada 앞으로 나아가다 advance, go forward, to

araboda 알아보다 recognize, to

arachaeda 알아채다 notice, realise, be aware of, to

...arae ...아래 under

arae.e 아래에 below

araecheung 아래층 downstairs

araero 아래로 down, downward

areumdapda, areumdaun 아름답다, 아름다운 beautiful, pretty

-aseo/eoseo -아서/어서 (cause or reason)

-aseo/eoseo -아서/어서 (sequence)

asia 아시아 Asia

-at/eot- -았/었- (past-tense suffix)

B

bada 바다 ocean, sea

badadeurida 받아들이다 accept, to

badageobuk 바다거북 turtle (sea)

badatga 바닷가 beach

...bae ...배 times (multiplying)

bae 배 belly, abdomen, stomach

bae 배 ship, boat, ferry

bae.uda 배우다 learn, to

bae.uja 배우자 partner, spouse

baebureuda 배부르다 full, eaten one's fill

baechu 배추 Chinese cabbage

baedalhada 배달하다 deliver, to

baegopeuda, baegopeun 배고프다, 배고픈 hungry

baek 백 hundred

baekhwajeom 백화점 department store

baem 뱀 snake

baengman 백만 million

baeseolhada 배설하다 defecate, to

baesimwon 배심원 jury

baguni 바구니 basket

baji 바지 pants, trousers

bakda, balgeun 밝다, 밝은 light, bright

bakkat(jjok) 바깥(쪽) outside

...bakke ...밖에 out
bakkuda 바꾸다 change, switch, to (conditions, situations)
baksuchida 박수치다 clap, to
bakwi 바퀴 wheel
bal 발 foot
balgyeonhada 발견하다 discover, to
baljjeon 발전 development
baljjeonhada 발전하다 develop (happen), to
baljjeonsikida 발전시키다 develop, to
balkkarak 발가락 toe
balmok 발목 ankle
balmyeonghada 발명하다 invent, to
baltop 발톱 nail (toe)
balttal 발달 development
bam 밤 night
bame 밤에 at night
bamneukke 밤늦게 late at night
ban 반 half
banana 바나나 banana
banbaji 반바지 shorts (short trousers)
banbokhada 반복하다 repeat, to
bandae(ui) 반대 (의) opposite (contrary)
bandaehada 반대하다 object, oppose, protest, to
baneujilhada 바느질하다 sew, to
baneul 바늘 needle
baneung 반응 reaction, response
baneunghada 반응하다 react, response, reply, to
bang 방 room (in house)
bang.eohada 방어하다 defend (in war), to
bangbeop 방법 way, method, manner

banghae 방해 bother, disturbance, hindrance
banghaehada 방해하다 bother, disturb, hinder, to
banghak 방학 vacation (school)
banghyang 방향 direction
bangjihada 방지하다 prevent, to
bangmulgwan 박물관 museum
bangmun 방문 visit
bangmunhada 방문하다 visit, to pay a
bangsong 방송 broadcast
bangsonghada 방송하다 broadcast, to
banji 반지 ring (jewellery)
bansahada 반사하다 reflect, to
bap 밥 rice (cooked), meal
bappeuda, bappeun 바쁘다, 바쁜 busy (doing something)
barada 바라다 desire, hope, wish, to
barageonde 바라건대 hopefully
baram 바람 wind, breeze
bareumhada 발음하다 pronounce, to
baro geugeoyeyo! 바로 그거예요! exactly! just so!
baro jigeum 바로 지금 just now
batda 받다 receive, to
batjul 밧줄 rope
bawi 바위 rock
begae 베개 pillow
belteu 벨트 belt
beolda 벌다 earn, to
beolgeobeotda, beolgeobeoseun 벌거벗다/벌거벗은 naked
beolgeum 벌금 fine, penalty (punishment)

3

beolle

beolle 벌레 insect
beolsseo 벌써 already
beomin 범인 criminal
beon.gae 번개 lightning
beonho 번호 number
beonyeokhada 번역하다 translate, to
beop 법 laws, legislation
beoreut 버릇 habit
beoreuteopda, beoreuteomneun 버릇없다 /버릇없는 naughty
beorida 버리다 abandon, desert, throw away, throw out, to
beoseot 버섯 mushroom
beoseu 버스 bus
beoseu jeonggeojang 버스 정거장 bus station
beotda 벗다 take off (clothes), to
beoteo 버터 butter
beteunam 베트남 Vietnam
beullauseu 블라우스 blouse
beuraejieo 브래지어 bra
beureikeu 브레이크 brake
beureikeu bapda 브레이크 밟다 brake, to
beurokeolli 브로컬리 broccoli
bi 비 rain
bijjaru 빗자루 broom
bibeon 비번 day off
bidio (rekodeu) 비디오 (레코드) video recorder, VCR
bidio (teipeu) 비디오 (테이프) video cassette
biga oda 비가 오다 rain, to
bigyohada 비교하다 compare, to
bihaeng 비행 flight
bihaenggi 비행기 aeroplane, airplane, plane
bihanggong.upyeon 비항공 우편 surface mail
bija 비자 visa
bijeuniseu 비즈니스 business, trade

bilding 빌딩 building
billida 빌리다 borrow, to
billyeojuda 빌려주다 lend, to
bimil 비밀 secret
bimireul jikida 비밀을 지키다 secret, to keep a
binan 비난 attack (with words)
binanhada 비난하다 blame, accuse, to
binbeonhada, binbeonhan 빈번하다, 빈번한 frequent
binnada, binnaneun 빛나다, 빛나는 shiny
binteumeopda/binteumeomneun 빈틈없다/ 빈틈없는 tight
binu 비누 soap
biokhada, biokan 비옥하다, 비옥한 fertile
birok -(eu)l jirado 비록 -(으)ㄹ 지라도 though, although
birok -jiman 비록 -지만 though, although
bisang(satae) 비상(사태) emergency
biseo 비서 secretary
biseuket 비스켓 biscuit
biseuthada, biseutan 비슷하다, 비슷한 similar
bissada, bissan 비싸다, 비싼 expensive
bit 빗 comb
bit 빚 debt
bitjida 빚지다 owe, to
biutda 비웃다 laugh at, to
biyeolhada, biyeolhan 비열하다, 비열한 mean (cruel)
biyong 비용 cost, expense, fee
biyul 비율 percentage
...boda (deo) ...보다 (더) (more) than (comparison)
boda 보다 look at, watch, see, view, to

...boda ohiryeo ...보다 오히려 rather than...
bogo 보고 report
bogohada 보고하다 report, to
bogwanhada 보관하다 save, keep, to
boheom 보험 insurance
bohoguyeok 보호구역 reserve (for animals)
bohohada 보호하다 protect, to
boida 보이다 reveal (make visible), to
bojeung 보증 guarantee
bojeunghada 보증하다 guarantee, to
bokdo 복도 corridor
bokgwon 복권 lottery
bokjaphada, bokjapan 복잡하다, 복잡한 busy, crowded
bokjaphada, bokjapan 복잡하다, 복잡한 complicated
boksa 복사 copy, photocopy
boksahada 복사하다 copy, photocopy, to
bolpen 볼펜 ball point
bom 봄 spring (season)
bonaeda 보내다 send, to
bonaeda 보내다 spend (time), to
bonbu 본부 headquarters
bonggeup 봉급 salary
bonghada 봉하다 seal, to
bongtu 봉투 envelope
bonneung 본능 instinct
boseok 보석 jewellery
boseu 보스 boss
boseyo! 보세요! look!
botong 보통 normally, usually
botong(ui) 보통(의) regular, normal
botong(ui) 보통(의) usual, ordinary, average
boyeojuda 보여주다 show, to

bu 부 department
bu.eok 부엌 kitchen
bu.in 부인 madam (term of address)
bubun 부분 part (not whole)
bubunjeogeuro 부분적으로 partly
buchae 부채 fan (for cooling)
buchida 부치다 post, mail, to
budeureopda, budeureo.un 부드럽다, 부드러운 soft
bujang 부장 manager
butjapda 붙잡다 hold, grasp, to
bujok 부족 tribe
bukdongjjok 북동쪽 northeast
bukhan 북한 North Korea
bukjjok 북쪽 north
bukkeureopda, bukkeureowohada 부끄럽다/부끄러워하다 ashamed
bukseojjok 북서쪽 northwest
bul 불 fire
bul 불 light (lamp)
bulganeunghada/-han 불가능하다/-한 impossible
bulgyo 불교 Buddhism
bulgyosinja 불교신자 Buddhist
bulhaeng 불행 misfortune
bulhaenghada, bulhaeng 불행하다, 불행한 unhappy
bulhaenghagedo 불행하게도 unfortunately
bulkkonnori 불꽃놀이 fireworks
bullida, bullineun 불리다, 불리는 called, named
bullihada 분리하다 separate, to
bulpiryohada, bulpiryohan 불필요하다, 불필요한 unnecessary

bulppeobida, bulppeop(ui) 불법이다, 불법(의 illegal

bulpyeong 불평 complaint

bulpyeonghada 불평하다 complain, to

bultago itda 불타고 있다 on fire

bumbida, bumbineun 붐비다, 붐비는 crowded

bumo 부모 parents

bun 분 minute

bunbyeollyeok itda/inneun 분별력 있다/있는 sensible

bungdae 붕대 bandage

bunsilmul 분실물 lost property

bunwigi 분위기 atmosphere, ambience

bureo.um 부러움 envy

bureojida, bureojin 부러지다, 부러진 broken (of bones, etc.)

bureojyeo nagada 부러져나가다 broken off

bureopda, bureowohada 부럽다, 부러워하다 envious

bureuda 부르다 call, summon, to

bureujitda 부르짖다 cry out, to

burun 불운 bad luck

busang 부상 injury

busok 부속 part (of machine)

but 붓 brush

butakhada 부탁하다 ask for, request (informally), to

butakhamnida 부탁합니다 please (request for help)

butda 붓다 pour, to

butda 붙다 stick to, to

...buteo ...부터 from (time)

buyuhada, buyuhan 부유하다, 부유한 rich, wealthy, well off

byeo 벼 rice (plant)

byeok 벽 wall

byeol 별 star

byeollo 별로 not really, not particularly

byeong 병 bottle

byeong 병 disease, illness

byeong.won 병원 hospital

byeonhohada 변호하다 defend (with words), to

byeonhosa 변호사 lawyer

C

cha 차 tea

cha taewojum 차 태워줌 lift (ride in car)

cha.aek 차액 difference (discrepancy in figures)

chadanbong 차단봉 bar (blocking way)

chae.uda 채우다 fill, to

chaegim 책임 duty, responsibility

chaegim itda/inneun 책임 있다/있는 responsible, to be

chaek 책 book

chaeksang 책상 desk

chaempi.eon 챔피언 champion

chago 차고 garage (for parking)

chai 차이 difference (in quality)

chajaboda 찾아보다 look up (find in book), to

chamgahada 참가하다 participate, to

chamgireum 참기름 sesame oil

chamkkae 참깨 sesame seeds

chamoe 참외 melon

chamseokhada 참석하다 attend, to

chamyeohada 참여하다 go along, join in, to

changgu 창구 window (for paying, buying tickets)

changjohada 창조하다 create, to

changmun 창문 window (in house)

changnyukhada 착륙하다 land (plane), to

changpihada! 창피하다! shame: what a shame!

chanjang 찬장 cupboard

chanseong! 찬성! agreed!

chapssal 찹쌀 glutinous rice

charyang 차량 vehicle

charye 차례 turn (make a turn)

chaseon 차선 lane (of a highway)

chatda 찾다 find, seek, look for, search for, to

chejung 체중 weight

chejung.i julda 체중이 줄다 weight, lose, to

chejung.i neulda 체중이 늘다 weight, gain, to

chekeuhada 체크하다 check, verify, to

chekeumunui(ui) 체크무늬(의) checked (pattern)

cheobang(jeon) 처방(전) prescription

cheokchu 척추 spine

cheol 철 iron

cheoljjeohada/-han 철저하다, 철저한 complete (thorough)

cheoljjahada 철자하다 spell, to

cheolmul 철물 hardware

cheolssa 철사 wire

cheoltto 철도 railroad, railway

cheon 천 thousand

cheon.guk 천국 heaven

cheonam 처남 brother-in-law

cheoncheonhi 천천히 slowly

cheondung 천둥 thunder

cheongdong 청동 bronze

cheongguseo 청구서 invoice

cheonggyeol 청결 cleanliness

cheongsohada 청소하다 clean, to

cheonjang 천장 ceiling

...cheoreom ...처럼 like, as

...cheoreom boida ...처럼 보이다 look like, to

cheorihada 처리하다 sort out, deal with, to

cheorihaenaeda 처리해내다 manage, succeed, to

cheosinhada 처신하다 behave, to

cheot beonjjae 첫 번째 first

cheseu 체스 chess

cheung 층 floor

cheung 층 layer

...cheung jjari ...층 짜리 storey (of a building)

chida 치다 hit, strike, to

chijeu 치즈 cheese

chikkwa(uisa) 치과(의사) dentist

chil 칠 painting

chil 칠 seven

chilhada 칠하다 paint (house, furniture), to

chilsip 칠십 seventy

chima 치마 skirt

chimdae 침대 bed

chimdaesiteu 침대시트 bedsheet

chimgu 침구 bedding, bedclothes

chimsil 침실 bedroom

chincheok 친척 relatives, family

chingchan 청찬 praise

chingchanhada 청찬하다 praise, to

chingho 칭호 title (of person)

chin.gu 친구 friend

chinhada, chinhan 친하다, 친한 close together

chinjeolhada, chinjeolhan 친절하다, 친절한 kind (of persons)

chirwol 칠월 July

chiryo 치료 cure (medical)

chiryohada 치료하다 treat (medically), to

chissol 칫솔 toothbrush

chisu 치수 measurement

chiyak 치약 toothpaste

chodae 초대 invitation

chodaehada 초대하다 invite (formally), to

choegeun(e) 최근(에) lately

choeseoneul dahada 최선을 다하다 do one's best, to

choeso 최소 least (smallest amount)

chojohaehada, chojohaehaneun 초조해하다/-하는 nervous

chokollet 초콜렛 chocolate

chong 총 gun

chu.eok 추억 memories

chucheonhada 추천하다 recommend, to

chucheukhada 추측하다 guess, to

chuga(ui) 추가 (의) extra

chukchukhada/-han 축축하다, 축축한 damp

chukgu 축구 soccer

chukhahada 축하하다 celebrate, to

chukhahaeyo! 축하해요! congratulations!

chukje 축제 festival

chukso 축소 reduction

chulbal 출발 departure

chulcheo 출처 origin, source

chulgu 출구 exit, way out

chulpanhada 출판하다 publish, to

chulseokhada, chulseokan 출석하다, 출석한 present (here)

chum 춤 dance

chumchuda 춤추다 dance, to

chungbunhada, chungbunhan 충분하다, 충분한 enough

chungdol 충돌 collision

chungdolhada 충돌하다 collide, to

chunggo 충고 advice

chunggohada 충고하다 advise, to

chupda, chuun 춥다, 추운 cold

chwijik 취직 employment

chwimi 취미 hobby

chwisohada 취소하다 cancel, to

chyeobusuda 쳐부수다 defeat, to

D

da haetda 다 했다 have done something, to

da tada 다 타다 burned down, out

da.eum 다음 following

da.eum(ui) 다음(의) next (in line, sequence)

da.eumju 다음 주 next week

dachida, dachin 닫히다, 닫힌 closed, shut (door)

dachida, dachin 다치다, 다친 hurt, injured

dae.uhada 대우하다 treat (behave towards), to

daebu 대부 loan

daebubun 대부분 most (the most of)

daechehada 대체하다 replace, to

daechero 대체로 on the whole

daedanhada, daedanhan 대단하다, 대단한 great, impressive

daedap 대답 answer, response (spoken)

daedaphada 대답하다 answer, respond reply (spoken), to

daegakseon(ui) 대각선(의) diagonal

daegakseoneuro 대각선으로 diagonally

daegang 대강 roughly, approximately

daehak 대학 university

daehanminguk 대한민국 Korea

daehwa 대화 conversation

daejeophada 대접하다 treat (something special), to

daemeorida, daemeoriin 대머리이다, 대머리인 bald

daeryuk 대륙 continent

daesa 대사 ambassador

daesagwan 대사관 embassy

...daesine ...대신에 instead of

daetongnyeong 대통령 president

daeyang, 대양 ocean

daeyeongjeguk 대영제국 United Kingdom

dahaenghi 다행히 fortunately

daiamondeu 다이아몬드 diamond

dak 닭 chicken

dakgogi 닭고기 chicken meat

dakda 닦다 polish, to

dakda 닦다 wipe, to

dal 달 month

dal 달 moon

dalda, dan 달다, 단 sweet

dallida 달리다 run, to

dalseonghada 달성하다 attain, reach, to

dam 담 fence

dambae 담배 cigarette

dambae pida 담배 피다 smoke (tobacco), to

damda 닮다 resemble, to

damdanggwan 담당관 authority (person in charge)

damnyo 담요 blanket

dan hana(ui) 단 하나(의) single (only one)

dan.gye 단계 step

danchu 단추 button

dandanhada, dandanhan 단단하다, 단단한 hard, solid, firm

daneo 단어 word

danggeun 당근 carrot

danggida 당기다 pull, to

danghwanghada/-haehada 당황하다/-해하 embarrassed

danjeonghada, danjeonghan 단정하다, 단정한 neat, tidy

danji 단지 just, only, merely

dansikhada 단식하다 fast, to

dansunhada, dansunhan 단순하다, 단순한 plain (not fancy)

dapjang 답장 answer, response (written)

dapjanghada 답장하다 answer, respond reply (written), to

darabeorida, darabeorin 닳아버리다/닳아버린 worn out (clothes)

daranaeda 달아내다 weigh out, to

dareuda, dareun 다르다, 다른 different

dareun 다른 another, other (different)

dari 다리 bridge

dari 다리 leg

darida 다리다 iron (clothing), to

daseot 다섯 five

...daseu ...다스 dozen

dasi 다시 again
daso 다소 more or less
datda 닫다 close, shut, to
de.uda 데우다 heat, to
deo 더 more (comparative)
deo jeokda/jeogeun 더 적다/ 적은 less (smaller amount)
deo jota/jo.eun 더 좋다/좋은 better
deo maneun 더 많은 more of (things)
deo nappeuda/nappeun 더 나쁘다/나쁜 worse
deohada 더하다 add, to
deonjida 던지다 throw, to
deopda 덮다 cover, close, to
deopda, deo.un 덥다, 더운 hot (temperature)
deoreopda, deoreo.un 더럽 다, 더러운 dirty
deukjeom 득점 score
...deul ...들 (plural particle)
deulleuda 들르다 stop by, pay a visit, to
deumulda, deumun 드물다, 드문 rare, scarce
deung 등 back (part of body)
deung 등 lamp
deunggeup 등급 degree, level
deunggi upyeon 등기 우편 registered post
deungnokhada 등록하다 register, to
deureo.oda 들어오다 come in, to
deureogada 들어가다 enter, to
(deureo)ollida (들어)올리다 lift, raise, to
deureseu 드레스 dress, frock
deutda 듣다 hear, listen, to
dibidi 디비디 DVD
dijain 디자인 pattern, design
dijeoteu 디저트 dessert, sweet

diseukaunteu 디스카운트 discount
diseuket 디스켓 diskette
...do ...도 also, too
do 도 degrees (temperature)
...do ...do ...도 ...도 both...and
...do ...do -ji anta ...도 ...도 -지 않다 neither...nor
...do ...do anida ...도 ...도 ... 아니다 neither...nor
...do ttohan ...도 또한 as well
...do ttohan -ji anta ...도 또한 -지 않다 nor
...do ttohan ...anida ...도 또 한 ...아니다 nor
dobak 도박 gamble
dochak 도착 arrival
dochakhada 도착하다 reach, arrive, get, to
doduk 도둑 thief
doeda 되다 become, to
dogi itda/inneun 독이 있다/ 있는 poisonous
dogu 도구 tool, utensil, instrument
dogyo 도교 Taoism
dojeon 도전 challenge
dok(yak) 독(약) poison
dokan sul 독한 술 spirits, hard liquor
dokgam 독감 flu
doksin(ui) 독신(의) single (not married)
dol 돌 stone
dolboda 돌보다 look after, take care of, to
dolda 돌다 turn around, to
dollida 돌리다 steer, to
dollyeojuda 돌려주다 return, give back, to
domanggada 도망가다 run away, to
don 돈 money
...dong.an ...동안 during, for

E

dong.eopja 동업자 partner (in business)
dong.i 동의 agreement
dong.ihada 동의하다 agree, to
donggong 동공 pupil
donggul 동굴 cave
dongjak 동작 movement, motion
dongjeon 동전 coin
dongjjok 동쪽 east
dongmul 동물 animal
dongmurwon 동물원 zoo
dongnip(ui) 독립(의) independent
dongniphada, dongnipan 독립하다, 독립한 free, independent
dongnyo 동료 co-worker, colleague
dongsaeng 동생 younger brother or sister
dongsang 동상 statue
dopda 돕다 assist, help, to
doragada 돌아가다 go back, return, to
doraoda 돌아오다 come back, return, to
doro 도로 road
doseogwan 도서관 library
dosi 도시 city
dosi(ui) 도시(의) urban
doum 도움 assistance
dowajuseyo! 도와주세요! help!
du bae 두 배 double
du beonjjae 두 번째 second
dubu 두부 bean curd, tofu
dudeurida 두드리다 knock, to
dugo gada 두고 가다 leave behind by accident and go, to
dugo oda 두고 오다 leave behind by accident and come, to
duk 둑 bank (of river)

dukkeopda, dukkeo.un 두껍다, 두꺼운 thick (of things)
dul 둘 two
dul da 둘 다 both
dunggeulda, dunggeun 둥글다, 둥근 round (shape)
dungji 둥지 nest
dwaeji 돼지 pig
dwaejigogi 돼지고기 pork
dwi 뒤 back, rear, tail
dwie 뒤에 behind
...dwie 뒤에 (place) after
dwijibeojida, dwijibeojin 뒤집어지다, 뒤집어진 overturned, upside down
dwijipda 뒤집다 over: to turn over
dwiro 뒤로 backward
dwiro gada 뒤로 가다 reverse, back up, to
dwittaragada 뒤따라가다 follow behind, to

E

...e ...에 in (time, years)
...e ...에 in, at, on (location)
...e ...에 on (of dates)
...e ...에 to (destination)
...e daehae ...에 대해 about (regarding, concerning)
...e daehae malhada ...에 대해 말하다 talk about, to
...e daehae mureoboda ...에 대해 물어보다 ask about, to
...e daehae nonjaenghada ...에 대해 논쟁하다 fight over, to
...e dallyeo.itda ...에 달려있다 depend on, to
...e gakkaun/gakkai ...(에) 가까운/가까이 close to, nearby
...e gichohada/gichohan ...에 기초하다/기초한 based on
...e gwanhayeo ...에 관하여 regarding, concerning

E

...e iksukhada ...에 익숙하다 know, be acquainted with, to

...e oreuda ...에 오르다 climb up (hills, mountains), to

...e sokada ... 에 속하다 belong to

...e uihae ...에 의해 by (author, artist)

...e uihamyeon ...에 의하면 according to

...ege ...에게 to, toward (a person)

ellibeiteo 엘리베이터 elevator

elliteu 엘리트 elite

eneoji 에너지 energy

enjin 엔진 engine

eo.ullida, eo.ullineun 어울리다, 어울리는 fitting, suitable

-eo/a boda -어/아 보다 try out -ing

-eo/a deurida -어/아 드리다 (humble form of -어/아 주다)

-eo/a juda -어/아 주다 do something for another's benefit

-eo/a juseyo -어/아 주세요 please (request for something)

-eo/ado jota -어/아도 좋다 may, can, be allowed to

-eo/aya hada -어/아야 하다 must, have to, ought to

eodi(e) 어디(에) where

eodideunji 어디든지 anywhere, everywhere

eodiedo ...eopda 어디에도 ... 없다 nowhere

eodin.ga 어딘가 somewhere

eodiro gaseyo? 어디로 가세 요? where to?

eodupda, eoduun 어둡다, 어 두운 dark

eoeop 어업 fishery

eogida 어기다 offend, to

eoje 어제 yesterday

eokjehada 억제하다 hold back, restrain, to

eokkae 어깨 shoulder

eolda 얼다 freeze, to

eollida 얼리다 freeze, to

eolda, eon 얼다, 언 frozen

eolgul 얼굴 face

eollon 언론 press, journalism

eollonin 언론인 journalist

eolluk 얼룩 stain

eolmana maniyo? 얼마나 많 이요? how many?

eolmana oraeyo? 얼마나 오 래요? how long?

eolmayeyo? 얼마예요? how much?

eomeona, sesang.e! 어머나, 세상에! goodness!

eomeoni 어머니 mother

eomgyeokhada, eomgyeokan 엄격하다/엄격한 strict

eomuk 어묵 fish paste

eondeok 언덕 hill

eoneo 언어 language

eoneu 어느 which

eoneu geoyo? 어느 거요? which one?

eoneu jjokdo -ji anta 어느 쪽 도 -지 않다 neither

eoneu jjokdo ..anida 어느 쪽 도 .... 아니다 neither

eongdeong.i 엉덩이 bottom, buttocks

eongmang.ida, eongmang.in 엉망이다 in a mess

eonje 언제 when

eonni 언니 older sister (female's)

...eopda, ...eomneun, ...없다, ... 없는 less

eopseojida, eopseojin 없어 지다, 없어진 missing (absent)

...eopsi ... 없이 without

eoreum 얼음 ice

eoreun 어른 adult

eorida, eorin 어리다, 어린 young

eoridungjeolhada/-haehada
어리둥절하다/-해하다
puzzled
eorini 어린이 child (young
person)
eoriseokda, eoriseogeun
어리석다, 어리석은 stupid,
silly
eoryeopda, eoryeo.un 어렵
다, 어려운 difficult, hard
eoseo 어서 quickly
eoseo oseyo! 어서 오세요!
welcome!
-eoseo/aseo -어서/아서
(cause or reason)
-eoseo/aseo -어서/아서
(sequence)
eoseoyo! 어서요! come on!,
let's go!
-eot/at- -었/았- (past tense
suffix)
eotda 얻다 get, receive, to
eotteoke 어떻게 how
eotteon 어떤 what kind of?,
which?
eotteon 어떤 some
eotteon geot 어떤 것
something
eotteon saram 어떤 사람
somebody, someone
ereo 에러 error
esei 에세이 essay
...eseo ...에서 from (starting
point)
...eseo ...에서 in, at on
(location of action)
...eseo ...에서 of, from
eseukeolleiteo 에스컬레이터
escalator
-(eu)l geosida -(으)ㄹ 것이다
will, shall
-(eu)l jul alda -(으)ㄹ 줄 알다
know how to
-(eu)l jul moreuda -(으)ㄹ 줄
모르다 not know how to
-(eu)l su itda -(으)ㄹ 수 있다
can, be able to, be capable of

-(eu)l sudo itda -(으)ㄹ 수도
있다 could, might
-(eu)l ttae -(으)ㄹ 때 when,
at the time
-(eu)l ttaekkaji -(으)ㄹ 때까지
until
-(eu)l ttaemada -(으)ㄹ 때마
다 every time, whenever
-(eu)l yeoyuga itda -(으)ㄹ 여
유가 있다 afford, to
-(eu)l/(eu)n/neun+(object)
-(으)ㄹ/(으)ㄴ/는+(사물)
the object which
-(eu)l/(eu)n/neun+(person)
-(으)ㄹ/(으)ㄴ/는+(사람)
the person who
...eul/reul ...을/를 (object
particle)
...eul/reul tonghayeo ...을/를
통하여 through, past
...eul/reul je.oehago ...을/를
제외하고 except
...eul/reul geochyeoseo ...을/
를 거쳐서 via
...eul/reul teul tonghayeo
...을/를 통하여 way: by way
of
...eul/reul uisikhada ...을/를
의식하다 conscious of, to be
...eul/reul wihan ...을/를 위
한 for
-(eu)lkkayo? -(으)ㄹ까요?
shall I/we? do you think?
eumak 음악 music
eumnyo 음료 drink,
refreshment
eumnyosu 음료수 soft drink
eumseong mesiji 음성 메시
지 voice mail
eumsik 음식 food
-eumyeon -(으)면 if, when
(condition)
eun 은 silver
-(eu)n ihuro -(으)ㄴ 이후로
since
-(eu)n jeogi itda -(으)ㄴ 적이
있다 ever, to have done

E

...eun/neun ... 은/는 as for, speaking of (topic marker)

-(eu)n/neun che hada -(으)ㄴ/는 체 하다 pretend, to

-(eu)n/neun/(eu)l+(object) -(으)ㄴ/는/(으)ㄹ+ (사물) the object which

-(eu)n/neun/(eu)l+(person) -(으)ㄴ/는/(으)ㄹ+ (사람) the person who

-(eu)nde/neunde -(으)ㄴ데/는데 (background information)

eunhaeng 은행 bank (finance)

-(eu)p sida -(으)ㅂ시다 let's (suggestion)

-(eu)reo -(으)러 in order to

...(eu)ro ...(으)로 toward, to (direction)

...(eu)ro ...(으)로 with (by means of)

...(eu)ro boida ...(으)로 보이다 look, seem, appear, to

...(eu)ro hyanghada ...(으)로 향하다 head for, toward, to

-(eu)ryeogo hada -(으)려고 하다 intend, mean, to

-(eu)seyo -(으)세요 (honorific polite ending)

-(eu)si -(으)시 (subject honorific suffix)

G

ga bonjeogi itda 가 본적이 있다 have been somewhere, to

ga.eul 가을 autumn, fall

...ga/i ...가/이 (subject marker)

-ga/i eopda/eomneun -가/이 없다/없는 lacking

gabang 가방 bag

gaboda 가보다 go around, visit, to

gabyeopda, gabyeo.un 가볍다, 가벼운 light (not heavy/severe)

gachi 가치 value, good

gachi gada 같이 가다 accompany, to

gachi itda 가치 있다 worth, to be

gada 가다 go, to

gadeuk chada/chan 가득 차다/찬 full

...gae ...개 item, piece, individual thing

gae 개 dog

gaein(ui) 개인(의) individual

gaeksil 객실 room (in hotel)

gage 가게 shop, store

gageum(nyu) 가금(류) poultry

gagu 가구 furniture

gajyeogada 가져가다 take, remove, to

gagyeok 가격 price, value (cost)

gaideu 가이드 guide, lead

gaiphada 가입하다 join, go along, to

gajang 가장 most (superlative)

gajang nappeuda/nappeun 가장 나쁘다/나쁜 worst

gajangjari 가장자리 border, edge

gajeonghada 가정하다 suppose, to

gaji 가지 branch

gaji 가지 eggplant, aubergine

gajigo nolda 가지고 놀다 play around, to

gajjaida, gajja(ui) 가짜이다, 가짜(의) false (imitation)

gajok 가족 family

gajuk 가죽 leather

gajyeo.oda 가져오다 bring, fetch, carry, to

gajyeogada 가져가다 carry, to

gakgak(ui) 각각(의) each, every, separate

...gakkai(e) ...가까이 (에) around, nearby

gakkaun geori 가까운 거리 walking distance

gakkawojida 가까워지다 approach (in time), to

gakkeum 가끔 sometimes, from time to time, occasionally

galsaek(ui) 갈색(의) brown

gamgagi eopda/eomneun 감각이 없다/없는 numb

gamgi 감기 cold, flu

gamgyullyu 감귤류 citrus

gamja 감자 potato

gamjeong 감정 emotion

gamok 감옥 jail, prison

gamsahada 감사하다 thank, to

gamsahamnida! 감사합니다! thank you!

gamtanhada 감탄하다 admire, to

gamum 가뭄 drought

gamyeomsikida 감염시키다 infect

gamyeon 가면 mask

gan 간 liver

gananhada, gananhan 가난하다, 가난한 poor

gandanhada, gandanhan 간단하다, 간단한 brief, short, simple

ganeudarata, ganeudaran 가느다랗다, 가느다란 slender

ganeun gire 가는 길에 on the way

ganeunghada, ganeunghan 가능하다, 가능한 possible

gang 강 river

gang.ui 강의 lecture, classes (at university)

gang.yohada 강요하다 force, compel, to

gangcheol 강철 steel

gangdo, doduk 강도, 도둑 burglar

gangnangkong 강낭콩 kidney beans

gangsa 강사 lecturer (at university)

ganhosa 간호사 nurse

ganjang 간장 soy sauce

ganpan 간판 signboard

gap 값 cost, price

gapjagi 갑자기 suddenly

garaipda 갈아입다 change, switch (clothes), to

gareuchida 가르치다 teach, to

garu 가루 powder

gaseum 가슴 chest (breast)

gasollin 가솔린 gasoline

gatda, gateun 같다, 같은 equal, identical, same, alike

gaunde 가운데 middle, center

gawi 가위 scissors

ge 게 crab

-ge -게 (adverbial suffix)

-ge boida -게 보이다 look, seem, appear, to

-ge hada -게 하다 let, allow, to

ge.eureuda, ge.eureun 게으르다, 게으른 lazy

geo.ul 거울 mirror

gedaga 게다가 besides, in addition

geim 게임 game

geo.i 거의 almost, nearly

geo.i -ji anta 거의 -지 않다 hardly, rarely, seldom

geo.i eopda/eomneun 거의 없다/없는 few

geo.in 거인 giant

geobuk 거북 turtle (land)

geochilda, geochin 거칠다, 거친 rough

geodaehada, geodaehan 거대하다, 거대한 huge

geogi 거기 there

G

geojeol 거절 refusal
geojeolhada 거절하다 decline, refuse, reject, to
geojinmalhada 거짓말 하다 lie, tell a falsehood, to
geojisida, geojit(ui) 거짓이다, 거짓(의) false (not true)
geokjeonghada 걱정하다 worry, to
geokkuro(ui) 거꾸로(의) reversed, backwards
geolda 걸다 hang, to
geolsang 걸상 stool
geommeokda/geommeogeun 겁먹다, 겁먹은 frightened
geomsahada 검사하다 test, to
geomtohada 검토하다 examine, to
geon.ganghada, geon.ganghan 건강하다, 건강한 healthy
geonbae! 건배! cheers!
geonchuk 건축 architecture
geonjohada, geonjohan 건조하다, 건조한 dry (weather)
geonneoda 건너다 cross, go over, to
geonneopyeone 건너편에 across from
geonneoseo 건너서 across
georaehada 거래하다 trade, exchange, to
georeoseo 걸어서 on foot
geori 거리 distance
geori 거리 street
georonhada 거론하다 bring up (topic), to
geotda 걷다 walk, to
geowi 거위 goose
-get- -겠- may, would (conjecture)
-get- -겠- would (intention)
geu 그 he, him
geu (geot) 그(것) that (near listener)

geu dong.an(e) 그 동안(에) meanwhile
geu hue 그 후에 afterwards, then
geu isang.ui 그 이상의 further, additional
geu yeoja 그 여자(의) she, her
geu yeoja.ui (geot) 그 여자의 (것) her (hers)
geu.ui 그의 his
geubakke 그밖에 else, anything else
geudeul 그들 they, them
geudeurui (geot) 그들의 (것) their (theirs)
geujeokke 그저께 day before yesterday
geukdoro 극도로 extremely
geukjang 극장 theater (drama)
geuljja 글자 character (written)
geum 금 gold
geumaek 금액 amount
geumanduda 그만두다 stop, cease, quit, to
geumanduseyo! 그만두세요! stop it!
geumhada 금하다 forbid, to
geumi gada/gan 금이 가다/ 간 cracked
geumjidoeda, geumjidoen 금지되다, 금지된 forbidden
geumsok 금속 metal
geumul 그물 net
geumyoil 금요일 Friday
geun.geo 근거 basis
geuncheo(e) 근처(에) around here
geuneul 그늘 shade
geunmyeonhada/-han 근면 하다/-한 hardworking, industrious
geunyuk 근육 muscle
geuraedo 그래도 nevertheless

geuraeseo 그래서 so, therefore, thus

geureochi aneumyeon 그렇지 않으면 or else, otherwise

geureochiman 그렇지만 but, however (conjunction)

geureoji maseyo! 그러지 마세요! don't!

geureoke haseyo 그렇게 하세요 please (go ahead)

geureomeuro 그러므로 therefore

geureomyeon 그러면 then

geureomyo! 그럼요! indeed!

geureon 그런 such

geureona 그러나 however, but

geureonde 그런데 by the way

geurida 그리다 draw, paint (a painting), to

geurigo 그리고 and

geurim 그림 picture, drawing, painting

geurimja 그림자 shadow

geuriwohada 그리워 하다 miss (loved one), to

geurup 그룹 group

geuttae 그때 then

-gi -기 (nominalizer)

-gi jeone -기 전에 before -ing

-gi sijakhada -기 시작하다 begin to

-gi ttaemune -기 때문에 because, since

-gi wihaeseo -기 위해서 in order that, so that

gi.eok 기억 memories

gi.eokhada 기억하다 remember, to

gibonjeogida, gibonjeogin 기본적이다, 기본적인 basic

gibun 기분 mood

gibun jota/jo.eun 기분 좋다/좋은 pleasant

gibun sanghage hada 기분 상하게 하다 offend, to

gibuni sanghada/sanghan 기분이 상하다/상한 upset, unhappy

gicha 기차 train

gicharo 기차로 by rail

gichim 기침 cough

gichimhada 기침하다 cough, to

gicho 기초 base, foundation, bottom

gidaehada 기대하다 expect, to

gidarida 기다리다 wait for, to

gidohada 기도하다 pray, to

gidokgyo 기독교 Christianity

gidokgyosinja 기독교신자 Christian

gidomun 기도문 prayer

gidung 기둥 post, column

gigan 기간 period (of time)

gigeum 기금 funds, funding

gigeun 기근 famine

gigye 기계 machine

gigyeryu 기계류 machinery

gihoe 기회 chance, opportunity

gihu 기후 climate

gija 기자 reporter

gilda, gin 길다, 긴 long (length)

gildeuryeojida/-yeojin 길들여지다/-여진 tame

gin.geuphada, gin.geupan 긴급하다, 긴급한 urgent

ginjang.eul pulda 긴장을 풀다 relax, to

ginjanghada, ginjanghan 긴장하다, 긴장한 tense

ginyeommul 기념물 monument

ginyeompum 기념품 souvenir

gipda, gipeun 깊다, 깊은 deep

gippal 깃발 flag

G

gippeuda, gippeohada 기쁘다, 기뻐하다 pleased

gippeuda, gippeun 기쁘다, 기쁜 glad

gippeum 기쁨 joy

gireul ilta/ireun 길을 잃다/잃은 lost (can't find way)

gireum 기름 oil

giri 길이 length

-giro hada -기로 하다 agree to do something, to

-giro hada -기로 하다 decide to, set to

gisa 기사 article (in newspaper)

gisa 기사 engineer

...go hada ...고 하다 that (introducing a quotation)

-go itda -고 있다 be -ing

-go naseo -고 나서 after -ing

-go sipda -고 싶다 want to

goa 고아 orphan

goche 고체 solid

gochida 고치다 correct, to

gochida 고치다 fix, repair, mend, to

gochu 고추 chilli pepper

gochujang 고추장 chilli paste

godae(ui) 고대(의) ancient

gogi 고기 meat

gogi japda 고기 잡다 fish, to

gogi wanja 고기 완자 meatball

gohwan 고환 testicles

gojangnada 고장나다 break down (car, machine), to

gojangnada, gojangnan 고장나다/고장난 broken, does not work

gojip seda/sen 고집 세다/센 stubborn, determined

goksik 곡식 grain

golchi apeuda/apeun 골치 아프다/아픈 troublesome

golmokgil 골목길 alley, lane

golpeu 골프 golf

golttongpum 골동품 antiques

gomapda, gomaun 고맙다, 고마운 grateful

gomapdago jeonhada 고맙다고 전하다 say thank you, to

gompang.i 곰팡이 fungus

gomu 고무 rubber

gong 공 ball

gong 공 zero

gong.won 공원 gardens, park

gong.ye 공예 crafts

gong.yega 공예가 crafts person

gongbuhada 공부하다 study, learn, to

gongchaek 공책 notebook

gonggan 공간 room, space

gonggeuphada 공급하다 provide, to

gonggi 공기 air

gonggong(ui) 공공(의) public

gonggyeok 공격 attack (in war)

gonghang 공항 airport

gongjang 공장 factory

gongjeonghada/-han 공정하다/-한 just, fair

gongmul 곡물 corn, grain

gongmuwon 공무원 officials (government)

gongsanghada 공상하다 daydream, to

gongsik(ui) 공식(의) official, formal

gongsonhada, gongsonhan 공손하다, 공손한 polite

gongteo 공터 field, empty space

gong.won 공원 park

-gonhaetda -곤했다 used to do something

goreuda 고르다 select, to

gosohada 고소하다 accuse, to

gosokdoro 고속도로 highway

G

got 곧 at once, immediately, soon
got hoebokhaseyo! 곧 회복하세요! get well soon!
gotong 고통 suffering
goyang.i 고양이 cat
goyohada, goyohan 고요하다, 고요한 silent, still, quiet, calm
goyonghada 고용하다 employ, hire, to
goyongju 고용주 employer
gu 구 nine
gugyeonghada 구경하다 watch (show, movie), to
gujohada 구조하다 rescue, to
guk 국 broth, soup
gukga 국가 nation, country
gukga(ui) 국가(의) national
gukhoe 국회 parliament
gukja 국자 dipper, ladle
gukjejeogida, gukje(jeogin) 국제적이다/국제(적인) international
gukjeok 국적 nationality
guksu 국수 noodles
gul 굴 oyster
gumeong 구멍 hole
gundae 군대 troops
gung 궁 palace
gunin 군인 soldier
gunsa(ui) 군사(의) military
gupda 굽다 bake, roast, grill, to
guri 구리 copper
gusip 구십 ninety
guun 구운 baked, roasted, grilled, toasted
guwol 구월 September
gwa 과 lesson, department
...gwa/wa ...과/와 and
...gwa/wa bigyohaeseo ...과/와 비교해서 compared with
gwabu 과부 widow

gwaenchanayo! 괜찮아요! don't mention it!, you're welcome!
gwaenchanta 괜찮다 okay
gwahak 과학 science
gwail 과일 fruit
gwaja 과자 confectionery, biscuit, cookie, cracker
gwallichaegimja 관리책임자 manager
gwallyeondoeda/-doen 관련되다/-된 involved
gwan.gwanggaek 관광객 tourist
gwangjang 광장 square, town square
gwan.gye 관계 relationship
gwanse 관세 duty (import tax)
gwanseup 관습 custom, tradition
gwansimi itda/inneun 관심이 있다/있는 interested in
gwi 귀 ear
gwibin 귀빈 guest of honor
gwiga meokda/meogeun 귀가 먹다/먹은 deaf
gwigeori 귀걸이 earrings
gwihage yeogida 귀하게 여기다 value, to
gwijunghada, gwijunghan 귀중하다, 귀중한 precious
gwisin 귀신 ghost
gwiyeopda, gwiyeo.un 귀엽다, 귀여운 cute
gwolli 권리 rights
gwonhan 권한 authority (power)
gyedan 계단 stairs, steps
gyegeup 계급 class, category
gyegok 계곡 valley
gyehoek 계획 plan
gyehoekhada 계획하다 plan, to
gyejeol 계절 season
gyeo.ul 겨울 winter

gyeo.u 겨우 barely
gyeokda 겪다 suffer, undergo, to
gyeolbaekhada, gyeolbaekan 결백하다, 결백한 innocent
gyeolgwa 결과 effect, result
gyeolgwaroseo 결과로서 resulting from, as a result
gyeolham 결함 defect
gyeolhonhada 결혼하다 marry, get married, to
gyeolhonhada, gyeolhonhan 결혼하다, 결혼한 married
gyeolhonsik 결혼식 wedding
gyeoljjeong 결정 decision
gyeoljjeonghada 결정하다 decide, to
gyeolko -ji anta 결코 -지 않다 never
gyeolko ...anida 결코 ...아니다 never
gyeolseokhada, gyeolseokan 결석하다, 결석한 absent
gyeonbon 견본 sample
gyeong.u 경우 case
gyeongchal 경찰 police
gyeongchalgwan 경찰관 police officer
gyeongchalseo 경찰서 police station
gyeongchi 경치 scenery, view
gyeonggijang 경기장 field, sports ground
(gyeonggireul)hada (경기를) 하다 play, to
gyeonggo 경고 warning
gyeonggohada 경고하다 warn, to
gyeonggye 경계 boundary, border (between countries)
gyeongheom 경험 experience
gyeongheomhada 경험하다 experience, to
gyeonghohada 경호하다 watch over, guard, to

gyeongjaeng 경쟁 competition
gyeongjaenghada 경쟁하다 compete, to
gyeongjaengsangdae 경쟁상대 rival
gyeongje 경제 economy
gyeongjejeogida/-jeogin 경제적이다/-적인 economical
gyeongmaehada 경매하다 auction, to
gyeongmaero pallida 경매로 팔리다 auctioned off
gyeongnyeohada 격려하다 encourage, to
gyeongnyeok 경력 career
gyeongsa 경사 slope
gyeran 계란 egg
gyesan.gi 계산기 calculator
gyesanhada 계산하다 calculate, to
gyesanseo 계산서 bill
gyesokhada 계속하다 continue, to
gyocha(ro) 교차(로) intersection
gyohoe 교회 church
gyohwanhada 교환하다 exchange (money, opinions), to
gyosu 교수 professor, lecturer
gyotong 교통 traffic
gyoyuk 교육 education
gyoyukhada 교육하다 educate, to
gyuchik 규칙 rules

H

hada 하다 do, perform an action, to
hadeudiseukeu 하드디스크 hard disk
hae 해 harm
hae.oe(ui) 해외(의) overseas
hae.oe.e(seo) 해외에(서) abroad

haeboda 해보다 try, to
haegohada 해고하다 fire someone, to
haegyeolhada 해결하다 resolve solve (a problem), to
haehyeop 해협 strait
haemul 해물 seafood
haendeupon 핸드폰 cell phone, mobile phone
haeng.uneul bimnida! 행운을 빕니다! good luck!
haengbangbulmyeongdoeda/ -deon 행방불명되다/-된 missing (person)
haengbokhada, haengbokan 행복하다, 행복한 happy
haengdong 행동 action
haenghada 행하다 act, to
haengsa 행사 event
haeropda, haero.un 해롭다, 해로운 harmful
haeppit 햇빛 sunlight
...hago ...하고 with (along)
hain 하인 servant
hakgyo 학교 school
haksaeng 학생 student, schoolchild, pupil
halmeoni 할머니 grandmother
haltta 핥다 lick, to
hamkke 함께 together
hamnijeogida/-jeogin 합리적 이다/-적인 reasonable, sensible
han ssang 한 쌍 pair of, a
hanguk 한국 Korea
han.gugeo 한국어 Korean
han.guk saram 한국 사람 Korean
hana 하나 one
hana deo 하나 더 another (same again)
hanbamjjung 한밤중 midnight
haneul 하늘 sky
haneunim 하느님 God

hang.uihada 항의하다 protest, to
hanggong.upyeon 항공우편 airmail
hanggu 항구 harbor, port
hanghaehada 항해하다 sail, to
hangmun 항문 anus
hangsang 항상 always
...hante ...한테 to (a person/animal)
...hanteseo ...한테서 from (a person/animal)
hapbeopjeogida, hapbeopjeogin 합법적이다 /합법적인 legal
hapdanghan seoneseo 합당 한 선에서 within reason
hapgye 합계 total
hapgyeokhada 합격하다 pass (exam), to
hapseong(ui) 합성(의) synthetic
hapum 하품 yawn
harabeoji 할아버지 grandfather
haru.ui 하루의 daily
hayata, hayan 하얗다, 하얀 white
heobeokji 허벅지 thigh
heoga 허가 licence, permit
heon geum 헌금 offering (church)
heorakhada 허락하다 allow, permit, to
heuk 흙 earth, soil
heundeulda 흔들다 shake something, swing, wave, to
heundeulheundeulhada/-han 흔들흔들하다/-한 loose (wobbly)
heungjeonghada 흥정하다 bargain, to
heunhada, heunhan 흔하다, 흔한 common, frequent
heurida, heurin 흐리다, 흐린 cloudy, overcast, dull

H

him 힘 force, power, strength

himitda, himinneun 힘 있다, 힘 있는 powerful

himjjul 힘줄 tendon

himseda, himsen 힘 세다, 힘 센 strong

hisaeng 희생 sacrifice

hisaenghada 희생하다 sacrifice, to

hoebokdoeda 회복되다 get better, be cured, to

hoebokhada, hoebokan 회복하다, 회복한 recovered

heon.geum 헌금 offering

hoesa 회사 company, firm

hoesaek(ui) 회색(의) grey

hoewon 회원 member

hoju 호주 Australia

hoju saram 호주 사람 Australian

hojumeoni 호주머니 pocket

hol 홀 hall

hollanseureopda 혼란스럽다 confused (in a mess)

hollansikida 혼란시키다 confuse, to

hollansikineun 혼란시키는 confusing

hondonghada 혼동하다 confused (mentally)

hondongsikida 혼동시키다 confuse, to

hondongsikineun 혼동시키는 confusing

hongkong 홍콩 Hong Kong

hongsu 홍수 flood

honja(seo) 혼자(서) alone

honjadoeda, honjadoen 혼자되다, 혼자된 widowed

honjaitda 혼자 있다 alone

horabi 홀아비 widower

horang.i 호랑이 tiger

hosu 호수 lake

hotel 호텔 hotel

huchu 후추 pepper, black

...hue ...후에 (time) after

huhoehada 후회하다 regret, to

hullyeon 훈련 training

humchida 훔치다 steal, to

hwa 화 anger

hwabun 화분 pot

hwachanghada/-han 화창하다/-한 sunny

hwajangsil 화장실 toilet, restroom, bathroom

hwakdaehada 확대하다 enlarge, to

hwakgohada/-han 확고하다/-한 determined, stubborn, firm

hwakjanghada 확장하다 expand, grow larger, to

hwaksilhada, hwaksilhan 확실하다, 확실한 certain, sure

hwalttong 활동 activity

hwan.gyeong 환경 environment, the

hwanada, hwanan 화나다, 화난 angry, cross

hwanghon 황혼 dusk

hwanja 환자 patient (doctor's)

hwanjeonhada 환전하다 change, exchange (money), to

hwannyul 환율 rate of exchange (for foreign currency)

hwanyeonghada 환영하다 welcome, to

hwasan 화산 volcano

hwasang 화상 burn (injury)

hwayoil 화요일 Tuesday

hwiballyu 휘발유 petrol

hyang 향 incense

hyangnyo 향료 spices

hyangsu 향수 perfume

hyangsuppyeong 향수병 homesickness

hyeo 혀 tongue

hyeomui 혐의 suspicion
hyeon.geum 현금 cash, money
hyeon.geumeuro bakkuda 현금으로 바꾸다 cash a check, to
hyeondae(ui) 현대(의) modern
hyeong 형 older brother (male's)
hyeongbu 형부 brother-in-law
hyeongje 형제 brother, sibling
hyeongseonghada 형성하다 shape, form, to
hyeongsu 형수 sister-in-law
hyeonjae 현재 at the present moment
hyeonmyeonghada, hyeonmyeonghan 현명하다/-한 wise
hyeonsanghada 현상하다 develop (film), to
hyu.ga 휴가 holiday, vacation (a period of time)
hyu.il 휴일 holiday (a day off)

i 이 this, these
i 이 tooth, teeth
i 이 two
i ae/bun 이 애/분 this (person)
i aedeul/bundeul 이 애들/분들 these (person)
i meil 이 메일 email (message)
i meil bonaeda 이 메일 보내다 email, to
i meil juso 이 메일 주소 email address
...i/ga ...이/가 (subject marker)
...i/ga eopda/eomneun ...이/가 없다/없는 lacking

ibalsa 이발사 barber
ibeo boda 입어 보다 try on (clothes), to
ichyeojida, ichyeojin 잊혀지다, 잊혀진 forgotten
...ieyo/yeyo ...이에요/예요 be (copula, polite ending)
igeot 이것 this (object)
igeotdeul 이것들 these (object)
igida 이기다 beat, win, defeat, to
igyeonaeda 이겨내다 overcome, to
ihaehada 이해하다 understand, to
ihonhada 이혼하다 divorce, to
ihonhada, ihonhan 이혼하다, 이혼한 divorced
...ihu ...이후 since
iik 이익 profit
ija 이자 interest (money)
ijeon(ui) 이전(의) previous
ikda 읽다 read, to
ikda, igeun 익다, 익은 ripe, to become
iksahada 익사하다 drown, to
iksukhada 익숙하다 acquainted, to be
il 일 job, work, occupation
ilbanjeogeuro 일반적으로 generally
ilbanjeogida/-jeogin 일반적이다/-적인 general, all-purpose
ilbanmi 일반미 sticky rice
ilbon 일본 Japan
ilbon saram 일본 사람 Japanese
ilboneo 일본어 Japanese
ilchul 일출 sunrise
ilgan 일간 daily
ilgi 일기 diary, daybook
ilgop 일곱 seven
ilhada 일하다 work, to
ilheun 일흔 seventy

iljji 일지 diary, journal
ilmol 일몰 sunset
ilttan 일단 once
ima 이마 forehead
imdaehada 임대하다 rent, to
immyeong 임명 appointment
...imnida ...입니다 be
(copula, deferential ending)
imsi(ui) 임시(의) temporary
imsinhada, imsinhan 임신하
다, 임신한 pregnant
in.gan 인간 human
in.gongjeogida, in.gongjeogin
인공적이다/-적인 artificial
...(i)na ...eoneu han jjok
...(이)나 ... 어느 한 쪽 either
...inbun ...인분 portion, serve
indonesia 인도네시아
Indonesia
ingkeu 잉크 ink
in.gu 인구 population
injeonghada 인정하다
admit, confess, to
inkki itda/inneun 인기 있다/
있는 popular
innaesimitda/-inneun 인내심
있다/-있는 patient
inpeulleisyeon 인플레이션
inflation
insaeng 인생 lifetime
insahada 인사하다 greet, to
insamal 인사말 greetings
insang.eul juda 인상을 주다
impression, to make an
insangjeogida, insangjeogin
인상적이다, 인상적인
impressive
insik 인식 awareness
insikhada 인식하다 aware
inswaehada 인쇄하다 print,
to
inteonet 인터넷 Internet
ip 입 mouth
ip 잎 leaf
ipda 입다 wear, put on,
climb onto, into (clothes), to
ipgu 입구 entrance, way in

ipjangkkwon 입장권 ticket
(for entertainment)
ipsul 입술 lips
irang 이랑 with (more
casual than 하고)
ireobeorida 잃어버리다 lose,
mislay, to
ireobeorin 잃어버린 lost
(missing)
ireon 이런 this kind of
ireonada 일어나다 get up
(from bed), to
ireonada 일어나다 happen,
occur, to
ireoseoda 일어서다 stand
up, to
ireuda, ireun 이르다, 이른
early
ireum 이름 name, given
name
iri(ro) 이리(로) here
irwol 일월 January
iryoil 일요일 Sunday
isahada 이사하다 move, to
isanghada, isanghan 이상하
다, 이상한 strange
iseullamgyo 이슬람교
Islam
iseullamgyodo 이슬람교도
Muslim
isip 이십 twenty
isyu 이슈 issue
itda 있다 available (time,
material, person)
itda 있다 be, exist, to
itda 있다 have, own, to
itda 있다 there is, there are
itda 잊다 forget, to
itgehada 있게 하다 make
available (time, material,
person), to
iut(saram) 이웃(사람)
neighbor
iwol 이월 February
iyagi 이야기 story
(tale)
iyu 이유 reason

J

jabusim 자부심 pride
jada 자다 sleep, go to bed, to
jadong eungdapgi 자동 응답기 answering machine
jadongcha 자동차 automobile, car, motor vehicle
jadu 자두 plum
jae.eonaeda 재어내다 measure out, to
jaebaehada 재배하다 grow, cultivate, to
jaechaegi 재채기 sneeze
jaechaegihada 재채기하다 sneeze, to
jaechokhada 재촉하다 urge, push for, to
jaeda 재다 measure, to
jaem 잼 jam
jaemiitda, jaemiinneun 재미있다, 재미있는 funny, interesting
jaemiitge bonaeda 재미있게 보내다 fun, to have
jaenan 재난 disaster
jaengban 쟁반 tray
jaeryo 재료 material, ingredient
jaesan 재산 property
jagi 자기 self
jago itda 자고 있다 asleep
jagung 자궁 uterus
jagyeok 자격 qualification
jagyonghada 작용하다 function, to work
jajeon.geo 자전거 bicycle
jaju 자주 often
jajusaek(ui) 자주색(의) purple
jakda, jageun 작다, 작은 little, small, tiny, short (not tall)
jakdonghada 작동하다 work, function, to
jaket 자켓 coat, jacket
jakga 작가 writer
jakgok 작곡 composition (music)

jakgokhada 작곡하다 compose (music), to
jakseonghada 작성하다 fill out, form, to
jal 잘 well, good
jal doegireul barada 잘 되기를 바라다 best wishes
jal garago jeonhada 잘 가라고 전하다 say goodbye, to
jal haesseoyo! 잘 했어요! well done!
jal ikda/igeun 잘 익다/익은 well-cooked, well-done
jalmot 잘못 fault
jalsaenggida, jalsaenggin 잘생기다, 잘생긴 handsome
jamae 자매 sister
jamgeuda 잠그다 lock, to
jamgida, jamgin 잠기다, 잠긴 locked
jamkkanmanyo! 잠깐만요! moment (just a moment)!
jamot 잠옷 nightclothes
jamsi 잠시 short time, a moment
jamulsoe 자물쇠 lock
janchi 잔치 festival
jandon 잔돈 change, small
jang 장 sheet (of paper)
jang.ae 장애 handicap
jang.in 장인 father-in-law
janggap 장갑 gloves
janghakgeum 장학금 scholarship
jangmo 장모 mother-in-law
jangmun 작문 composition, writings
jangnankkam 장난감 toy
jangnyeon 작년 last year
jangnyesik 장례식 funeral
jangsigi manta/maneun 장식이 많다/많은 fancy
jangsik(mul) 장식(물) ornament
jangso 장소 place
janinhada, janinhan 잔인하다, 잔인한 cruel

J

japda 잡다 capture, catch, to
japji 잡지 magazine
jarada 자라다 grow, be growing (plant), to
jarangseureopda, jarangseureon 자랑스럽다/-스런 proud
jareogada 자러가다 go to bed, to
jareuda 자르다 cut, to
jari 자리 seat
jasin 자신 confidence
jasin itda 자신 있다 confidence, to have
jasinui 자신의 own, personal
jason 자손 descendant
(ja)su (자)수 embroidery
jayeon 자연 nature
jayeon(ui) 자연(의) natural
jayu 자유 freedom, liberty
jayuropda, jayuroun 자유롭다, 자유로운 free of restraints
je 제 I, my (humble form)
je sigane 제 시간에 on·time
je.an 제안 suggestion
je.anhada 제안하다 suggest, to
jeo.ul 저울 scales
je.uihada 제의하다 offer, suggest, to
jechulhada 제출하다 present, to
jegeohada 제거하다 get rid of, to
jehan 제한 limit
jehanhada 제한하다 limit, to
jeil 제일 most (superlative)
jeil jota/jo.eun 제일 좋다/좋은 best
jejohada 제조하다 manufacture, to
jemok 제목 title (of book, film)
jeo 저 I, me (humble form)
jeo 저 that, those
jeo ae/bun 저 애/분 that (person)

jeo aedeul/bundeul 저 애들/분들 those (person)
jeo geot 저 것 that (object)
jeo geotdeul 저 것들 those (object)
jeogeodo 적어도 at least
jeogi 저기 over there
jeojangdoeda, jeojangdoen 저장되다/저장된 preserved, cured
jeojanghada 저장하다 store, to
jeok 적 enemy
jeokda 적다 note down, to
jeokda, jeogeun 적다, 적은 little (not much)
jeokdanghada, jeokdanghan 적당하다, 적당한 appropriate
jeokdanghada, jeokdanghan 적당하다, 적당한 reasonable (price)
jeokdanghada, jeokdanghan 적당하다, 적당한 suitable, fitting
jeoksida 적시다 soak, to
jeol 절 temple
jeolmeum 젊음 youth (state of being young)
jeolmeuni 젊은이 youth (young person)
jeom 점 point, dot
jeomchajeogeuro 점차적으로 gradually
jeomjanta, jeomjaneun 점잖다, 점잖은 gentle
jeommuneu(ui) 점무늬(의) spotted (pattern)
jeompeuhada 점프하다 jump, to
jeomsim siksa 점심 식사 lunch, midday meal
jeomsim siksahada 점심 식사하다 lunch, to eat
jeomwon 점원 sales assistant, shopkeeper
jeonche 전체 entirety, whole

jeonche(ui) 전체(의) entire, whole, all of

...jeone ...전에 ago

jeone 전에 before (in time)

jeong.i 정의 justice

jeong.o 정오 noon, midday

jeong.won 정원 garden, yard

jeongbiso 정비소 garage (for repairs)

jeongbo 정보 information

jeongbu 정부 government

jeongchihak 정치학 politics

jeongdang 정당 party (political)

...jeongdo ...정도 about (approximately)

jeongdondoeda/-doen 정돈 되다/-된 orderly, organized

jeongdonhada 정돈하다 tidy up, to

jeonggeul 정글 jungle

jeonghada 정하다 fix (a time, appointment), to

jeonghwakhada, jeonghwakan 정확하다, 정 확한 exact

jeonghwakhi 정확히 exactly

jeon.gi 전기 electricity

jeon.gi(ui) 전기(의) electric

jeongjang 정장 suit, business

jeongjikhada, jeongjikan 정 직하다, 정직한 honest

jeongmal 정말 really, truly

jeongmaryo? 정말요? really?

jeongmyeon 정면 front

jeongnihada 정리하다 arrange, organize, to

jeongnyeol 정열 passion

jeongnyujang 정류장 stop (bus, train)

jeongsagakhyeong 정사각형 square (shape)

jeongsang 정상 peak, summit

jeongsangjeogida, jeongsangjeogin 정상이 다/정상적인 normal

jeonhwa batda 전화 받다 answer the phone, to

jeonhwa(gi) 전화(기) telephone

jeonhwabeonho 전화번호 telephone number

jeonhwahada 전화하다 ring, call dial (on the telephone), to

jeonhyeongjeogida/-jeogin 전형적이다/-적인 typical

jeonja jepum 전자 제품 appliance, electrical

jeonja(ui) 전자(의) electronic

jeonjaeng 전쟁 war

jeonjaenghada 전쟁하다 war, to make

jeonjaupyeon 전자우편 email (system)

jeonmun.ga 전문가 expert

jeonseol 전설 legend

jeontongjeok(in) 전통적(인) traditional

jeontu 전투 battle

jeonyeok 저녁 evening

jeonyeok siksa 저녁 식사 dinner, evening meal

jeonyeok siksahada 저녁 식사하다 dinner, to eat

jeopda 접다 fold, to

jeopgeunhada 접근하다 approach (in space), to

jeopsi 접시 dish, platter

jeopsibatchim 접시받침 tablemat

jeoreon 저런 that kind of

jeotda, jeojeun 젖다, 젖은 wet

jeotgarak 젓가락 chopsticks

jeseucheo 제스처 gesture

jeulgeopda, jeulgeo.un 즐겁 다, 즐거운 enjoyable

jeulgeopge bonaeda 즐겁게 보내다 enjoy oneself, to

J

jeulgida 즐기다 enjoy, to
jeung.o 증오 hatred
jeungga 증가 increase
jeunggahada 증가하다 increase, rise, to
jeunggeo 증거 proof
jeunggi 증기 steam
jeungmyeonghada 증명하다 prove, to
jeungmyeongseo 증명서 certificate
-ji aneumyeon -지 않으면 unless
-ji anta -지 않다 no, not (with verbs and adjectives)
-ji maseyo -지 마세요 Please don't
-ji motada -지 못하다 cannot
-ji anta -지 않다 not
jibang 지방 fat, grease
jibang 지방 region
jibe doraoda 집에 돌아오다 return home, to
jibe gada 집에 가다 go home, to
jibul 지불 payment
jibuldoeda, jibuldoen 지불되다, 지불된 paid
jibulhada 지불하다 pay, to
jibung 지붕 roof
jiburaek 지불액 payment
jichulgeum 지출금 expenses
jida 지다 lose, be defeated, to
jido 지도 map
jidohada 지도하다 lead (to be a leader), to
jidoja 지도자 leader
jigap 지갑 purse wallet (for money)
jigeop 직업 job, occupation, profession
jigeum 지금 now, at the present moment
jigeum dangjang 지금 당장 right now
jigu 지구 Earth, the world

jigwon 직원 staff
jijeokhada 지적하다 point out, to
jijeom 지점 branch
jijihada 지지하다 support, to
jijin 지진 earthquake
jikida 지키다 guard, keep, to
jiksagakhyeong 직사각형 rectangle
jilmun 질문 question
jiltu 질투 jealousy
jiltuhada, jiltuhaneun 질투하다, 질투하는 jealous
jim 짐 baggage, package, load
-jiman -지만 but
jinada, jinan 지나다, 지난 past, former
jinan bam 지난 밤 last night
jinan ju 지난 주 last week
jinchalhada 진찰하다 examine, to
jingmul 직물 fabric, textile
(jingmureul) jjada (직물을) 짜다 weave, to
jingmyeonhada 직면하다 face, to
jinhada, jinhan 진하다, 진한 thick (of liquids)
jinjja(ui) 진짜(의) genuine
jinju 진주 pearl
jinyeol 진열 display
jinyeolhada 진열하다 display, to
jip 집 home, house
jipjunghada 집중하다 concentrate, to
jipye 지폐 note (currency)
jipyeongseon 지평선 horizon
jiri(hak) 지리(학) geography
jiruhada, jiruhaehada 지루하다, 지루해하다 bored
jiruhada, jiruhan 지루하다, 지루한 boring, dull
jisihada 지시하다 instruct, tell to do something, to
jisik 지식 knowledge

jisokhada 지속하다 last, to
jitda 짓다 build, to
jiwi 지위 rank, station in life
jiyeok 지역 area, region
jiyeon 지연 delay
jiyeondoeda, jiyeondoen 지연되다, 지연된 delayed
-jiyo? -지요? isn't it?
jjada, jjan 짜다, 짠 salty
jjagi 짜기 weaving
jjajeung.i nada 짜증이 나다 annoyed
jjida, jjin 찌다, 찐 steamed
jjigae 찌개 soup (spicy stew)
jjinggeurida 찡그리다 frown, to
jjitda 찢다 tear, rip, to
jjochanaeda 쫓아내다 chase away, chase out, to
jjogaeda 쪼개다 break apart, to
jjok 쪽 side
jjotda 쫓다 chase, to
jjuk ttaragada 쭉 따라가다 follow along, to
joahada 좋아하다 like, care for, be fond of, be pleased by, to
joajida 좋아지다 get better, improve, to
jobu 조부 grandfather
jobumo 조부모 grandparents
...jochado ...조차도 even (also)
joechaekgameul neukkida 죄책감을 느끼다 feel guilty, to
jogak 조각 carving, sculpture
jogak 조각 piece, portion, section, cut, slice
jogakhada 조각하다 carve, sculpt, to
jogeum 조금 a little, bit
johwadoeda, johwadoen 조화되다, 조화된 harmonious
joka 조카 nephew

jokattal 조카딸 niece
jokkeon 조건 condition (pre-condition)
jokki 조끼 vest, undershirt
jollida, jollin 졸리다, 졸린 sleepy, tired
jomo 조모 grandmother
jon.gyeong 존경 respect
jon.gyeonghada 존경하다 respect, to
jong.eobwon 종업원 waiter, waitress
jong.i 종이 paper
jonggyo 종교 religion
jongnyu 종류 kind, type, sort
jonjaehada 존재하다 exist, to
jopda, jobeun 좁다, 좁은 narrow
joribeop 조리법 recipe
joriphada 조립하다 assemble, put together, to
josahada 조사하다 inspect, to
josang 조상 ancestor
josimhada 조심하다 to be careful
josimhaseyo! 조심하세요! careful!, look out!
jota 좋다 okay
jota, jo.eun 좋다, 좋은 good, fine
joyonghada, joyonghan 조용하다, 조용한 quiet
ju 주 week
jubu 주부 housewife
juchahada 주차하다 park (car), to
juda 주다 give, to
jugan 주간 weekly
jugeum 죽음 death
jugeup 주급 wages
jugida 죽이다 kill, murder, to
ju.in 주인 host
jujanghada 주장하다 insist, to
juje 주제 topic

J

jujeohada 주저하다 hesitate, to

jujeonja 주전자 jug, pitcher

jukda 죽다 die, to

jukda, jugeun 죽다, 죽은 dead

jul 줄 queue, line

julda 줄다 decrease, reduce, to

julmunui(ui) 줄무늬(의) striped

julseoda 줄서다 line up, queue, to

jumal 주말 weekend

jumin 주민 resident, inhabitant

jumokhada 주목하다 pay attention, to

jumun 주문 order (placed for food, goods)

jumunhada 주문하다 order something, to

junbi 준비 arrangements, planning

junbidoeda, junbidoen 준비 되다, 준비된 prepared, ready

junbihada 준비하다 prepare, arrange, get ready, to

junbisikida 준비시키다 prepare, make ready, to

jung.ang 중앙 center, middle

jung.ang(ui) 중앙(의) central

...jung.e(seo) ...중에(서) among

jung.yohada, jung.yohan 중 요하다, 중요한 important, major

jung.yoseong 중요성 importance

jungdaehada, jungdaehan 중 대하다, 중대한 serious, severe

junggan 중간 middle, center

junggugeo 중국어 Chinese

jungguk 중국 China

jungguk saram 중국 사람 Chinese

jungsim 중심 center, middle

jungsim(ui) 중심(의) central

jungsimji 중심지 center (of city)

jupda 줍다 pick up, lift (something), to

jurida 줄이다 decrease, lessen, reduce, to

juro 주로 mostly, mainly

jusa 주사 injection

jusahada 주사하다 inject, to

juso 주소 address

juwibaegyeong 주위배경 surroundings

...juwie ...주위에 around, round (surrounding)

juyohan 주요한 main, most important

juyuso 주유소 gasoline station, petrol station

jwi 쥐 rat

jyuseu 쥬스 juice

K

kadeu(nori) 카드(놀이) cards, game

kal 칼 knife

kambodia 캄보디아 Cambodia

kamera 카메라 camera

kapeteu 카페트 carpet

kaseteu 카세트 cassette

kaunteu 카운트 counter (for paying, buying tickets)

keikeu 케이크 cake, pastry

keojida 커지다 grow larger, to

keollipeullawo 컬리플라워 cauliflower

keompyuteo 컴퓨터 computer

keop 컵 cup, glass (for drinking)

keopi 커피 coffee

keoteun 커튼 curtain

keuda, keun 크다, 큰 big, large

keuraekeo 크래커 cracker, salty biscuit

ki 키 key (computer)
ki keuda/keun 키 크다/ 큰 tall
kibodeu 키보드 keyboard (of computer)
killogeuraem 킬로그램 kilogram
killomiteu 킬로미터 kilometer
kiseu 키스 kiss
kiseuhada 키스하다 kiss, to
kiwi 키위 kiwi fruit
kkadaropda, kkadaroun 까다롭다, 까다로운 fussy
kkae.eo itda 깨어 있다 awake
kkae.eo nada 깨어나다 awake, wake up, to
kkae.uda 깨우다 awaken, wake someone up, to
kkaejida, kkaejin 깨지다, 깨진 broken, shattered
kkaekkeuthada, kkaekkeutan 깨끗하다, 깨끗한 clean
kkaetteurida 깨뜨리다 break, shatter, to
...kkaji ...까지 until, by
kkalgae 깔개 mat
kkaman kong 까만 콩 black beans
kkamata, kkaman 까맣다, 까만 black
kkangtong 깡통 can, tin
...kke ...께 to (a person) (honorific of 에게, 한테)
kkeojida 꺼지다 go out (fire, candle), to
kkeojyeo itda 꺼져 있다 off (turned off)
kkeopjireul beotgida 껍질을 벗기다 peel, to
...kkeseo ...께서 (honorific subject particle)
kkeuda 끄다 off: switch off, turn off, to
kkeun 끈 string
kkeunjeok.kkeunjeokhada/-han 끈적끈적하다/-한 sticky

kkeunnada 끝나다 end, to
kkeunnada 끝나다 over, finished, done, complete, gone
kkeunnada, kkeunnan 끝나다, 끝난 closed (shop)
kkeunnaeda 끝내다 complete, to
kkeunnaeda 끝내다 end, finish off, to
kkeurida 끓이다 boil, to
kkeurin 끓인 boiled
kkeut 끝 tip, end, finish
kkochaeng.i 꼬챙이 skewer
kkok matda 꼭 맞다 fit, to
kkokdaegi 꼭대기 top
kkori 꼬리 tail
kkot 꽃 flower
kkotbyeong 꽃병 vase
kkul 꿀 honey
kkum 꿈 dream
kkumida 꾸미다 decorate, to
kkumkkuda 꿈꾸다 dream, to
kkyeo.anda 껴안다 embrace, to
ko 코 nose
ko golda 코 골다 snore, to
kokkiri 코끼리 elephant
kokkumeong 콧구멍 nostril
kokoneot 코코넛 coconut
koneo 코너 corner
kong 콩 bean
kossuyeom 콧수염 moustache
koteu 코트 coat, overcoat
kuki 쿠키 cookie, sweet biscuit
kyeoda 켜다 on: switch on, turn on, to
kyeojyeo itda 켜져 있다 on (turned on)

M

ma.eul 마을 village, town
ma.eum 마음 heart

ma.eum pyeonhada 마음 편하다 at home (feel)

ma.eumeul bakkuda 마음을 바꾸다 change one's mind, to

machan.gajiro 마찬가지로 likewise

machimnae 마침내 finally

machimpyo 마침표 period (end of a sentence)

madang 마당 courtyard

mae... 매... every

maebeon 매번 every time

maeda 매다 tie, to

maeje 매제 brother-in-law

maejin 매진 sold out

maekju 맥주 beer

maekkeureopda/-reo.un 매끄럽다/-러운 smooth (of surfaces)

maepda, mae.un 맵다, 매운 hot, spicy

maeryeokjeogida, maeryeokjeogin 매력적이다/-적인 attractive

maeteuriseu 매트리스 mattress

magae 마개 plug (bath)

maheun 마흔 forty

maineoseu 마이너스 minus

majak 마작 mah jong

majeun pyeon(ui) 맞은 편(의) opposite (facing)

majimak(ui) 마지막(의) final

makda, malgeun 맑다, 맑은 clear (of weather)

makdaegi 막대기 stick, pole

makhida, makin 막히다, 막힌 closed (road)

mal 말 horse

mal 말 language

maldatum 말다툼 quarrel

malhada 말하다 say, speak, talk, tell, mention, to

malleisia 말레이시아 Malaysia

mallida 말리다 dry, to

...man ...만 only

man 만 bay

man 만 ten thousand

mandeulda 만들다 make up, invent, to

mandeulda 만들다 make, to

mandu 만두 dumpling

maneul 마늘 garlic

maneun 많은 lots of

...mang ...망 network

mangchi 망치 hammer

manggajida, manggajin 망가지다/-진 spoiled (does not work)

manggo 망고 mango

manhwa 만화 cartoon

mani 많이 a lot

manil -(eu)myeon 만일 -(으)면 if

manjida 만지다 touch, to

manjokhada, manjokaehada 만족하다/-해하다 satisfied

manjoksikida 만족시키다 satisfy, to

mannada 만나다 meet, to

manta, maneun 많다, 많은 many, much

mareuda, mareun 마르다, 마른 dry

mareuda, mareun 마르다, 마른 thin (of persons)

maria 마리아 the Virgin Mary

maru 마루 floor

maryeonhada 마련하다 arrange, organize, to

masajihada 마사지하다 massage, to

masi nada 맛이 나다 taste (salty, spicy), to

masida 마시다 drink, to

masitda, masinneun 맛있다, 맛있는 delicious, tasty

mat 맛 taste

matboda 맛보다 taste (sample), to

matda, manneun 맞다, 맞는 correct

matgida 맡기다 leave behind for safekeeping, to
mauseu 마우스 mouse (computer)
mayak 마약 drug (recreational)
memareun 메마른 barren
memo 메모 note (written)
menyu 메뉴 menu
meogida 먹이다 feed, to
meokda 먹다 eat, to
meolda, meon 멀다, 먼 far
meomchuda 멈추다 stop, halt, to
meomureuda 머무르다 stay, remain, to
meong 멍 bruise
meonjeo 먼저 first, earlier, beforehand
meonji 먼지 dust
meori 머리 head
meori(karak) 머리(카락) hair
meot 몇 how many?, what...? (number)
meotjida, meotjin 멋지다, 멋진 wonderful, nice, beautiful
meriyaseu 메리야스 undershirt
meseukkeopda 메스껍다 sick, to be (vomit)
mesiji 메시지 message
mianhadago jeonhada 미안하다고 전하다 say sorry, to
mianhamnida! 미안합니다! sorry! excuse me! (apology)
michida, michin 미치다, 미친 mad, crazy, insane
mideum 믿음 belief, faith
miguk 미국 America, United States
miguk saram 미국 사람 American
milda 밀다 push, to
milkkaru 밀가루 flour
milsuhada 밀수하다 smuggle, to
minibeoseu 미니버스 minibus

minjok 민족 ethnic group
minjuju.i 민주주의 democracy
mirae 미래 future: in future
miri 미리 beforehand, earlier
misojitda 미소짓다 smile, to
mitda 믿다 believe, trust, to
miwohada 미워하다 hate, to
modeun 모든 all, every
modeun geot 모든 것 everything
modeun got 모든 곳 everywhere
modeun jongnyu.ui 모든 종류의 every kind of
modeun saram 모든 사람 everybody, everyone
modu 모두 all, altogether, in total
mo.euda 모으다 assemble, gather, to
mogi 모기 mosquito
moida 모이다 assemble, gather, to
mogyoil 목요일 Thursday
mogyok 목욕 bath
mogyokgaun 목욕가운 bathrobe
mogyokhada 목욕하다 bathe, take a bath, to
mogyoksil 목욕실 bathroom
mohohada, mohohan 모호하다, 모호한 vague
moim 모임 meeting
moja 모자 cap, hat
mok 목 neck
mok(gumeong) 목(구멍) throat
mokgeori 목걸이 necklace
mokgyeokhada 목격하다 witness, to
mokgyeokja 목격자 witness
mokjeok 목적 purpose
mokjeokji 목적지 destination
mokpyo 목표 goal
moksori 목소리 voice
mom 몸 body

mongmareuda, mongmareun 목마르다, 목마른 thirsty

moniteo 모니터 monitor (of computer)

morae 모래 sand

more 모레 day after tomorrow

mosida 모시다 serve, to

mot 못 can't

mot 못 nail (spike)

moteo 모터 motor, engine

motsaenggida, motsaenggin 못생기다, 못생긴 ugly

moyang 모양 form, shape

moyok 모욕 insult

moyokhada 모욕하다 insult someone, to

mudeom 무덤 grave

mudeopda, mudeo.un 무덥다, 무더운 humid

mueosideunji 무엇이든지 anything

mueot 무엇 what

muge 무게 weight

mugeopda, mugeo.un 무겁다, 무거운 heavy

mugereul dalda 무게를 달다 weigh, to

mugi 무기 weapon

mukda 묵다 stay overnight, to

mukda, mulgeun 묽다, 묽은 thin (of liquids)

mul 물 water

mulche 물체 object, thing

mulda 물다 bite, to

mulgeon 물건 thing

mulgyeolchida 물결치다 wave, to

mulkkogi 물고기 fish

mullon 물론 of course

mulso 물소 buffalo (water buffalo)

mumigeonjohada/-han 무미건조하다/-한 bland

mun 문 door, gate

mun.guryu 문구류 stationery

munhak 문학 literature

munhwa 문화 culture

munjang 문장 sentence

munje 문제 problem, question, trouble, matter

munjireuda 문지르다 scrub, to

munpeopp 문법 grammar

munseo 문서 document, letter

munui(ui) 무늬(의) patterned

mureoboda 물어보다 enquire, to

mureup 무릎 knee

muryehada, muryehan 무례하다, 무례한 impolite, rude

muryo(ui) 무료(의) free of charge

museo.um 무서움 fear

museopda, museo.un 무섭다, 무서운 terrible

museopda, museowohada 무섭다, 무서워하다 afraid, scared

museun irieyo? 무슨 일이에요? what happened?

musihada 무시하다 ignore, to

musikhada, musikan 무식하다, 무식한 ignorant

mutda 묻다 bury

muyeok 무역 trade, business

mwo hasigeyo? 뭐 하시게요? what for?

mworago hasyeosseoyo? 뭐라고 하셨어요? pardon me?

mworagoyo? 뭐라고요? what?

myeon 면 cotton

myeondohada 면도하다 shave, to

myeoneuri 며느리 daughter-in-law

myeong.ye 명예 honor

myeongbaekhada, myeongbaekan 명백하다/-한 obvious

myeongbaekhi 명백히 apparently

myeongdan 명단 list

myeonghwakhada, myeonghwakan 명확하다/-한 definite

myeongjeol 명절 holiday (festival)

myeongnyeong 명령 command, order

myeongnyeonghada 명령하다 order, command, to

myeonheojjeung 면허증 licence (for driving)

myeonjeop 면접 interview

myeot sarieyo? 몇 살이에요? how old?

myeot siyo? 몇 시요? what time?

myosahada 묘사하다 describe, to

N

na 나 I, me

na.ui 나의 (것) my, mine

nabang 나방 moth

nabi 나비 butterfly

nache 나체 nude

nae 내 I, my

nae 내 것 mine

nae.il 내일 tomorrow

naembi 냄비 pan, pot

naemsae 냄새 odor, bad smell

naemsaematda 냄새맡다 smell, to

naemsaenada 냄새나다 stink, smell, to

naengjanggo 냉장고 refrigerator

naengjanghada/-han 냉장하다/-한 chilled

naengnanbang 냉난방 air conditioning

naenyeon 내년 next year

naerida 내리다 get off (transport), to

naeseon 내선 extension (telephone)

nagada 나가다 go out, exit, to

nai 나이 age

nai manta/maneun 나이 많다/ 많은 old (of persons)

naillon 나일론 nylon

najung.e 나중에 later

najung.e bopsida! 나중에 봅시다! see you later!

nakje 낙제 failure (study)

nakjehada 낙제하다 fail, to

nal 날 day

nal (geosui) 날 (것의) raw, uncooked

nalda 날다 fly, to

nalgae 날개 wing

naljja 날짜 date (of the month)

nalkaropda, nalkaroun 날카롭다, 날카로운 sharp

nalssi 날씨 weather

nalssinhada, nalssinhan 날씬하다, 날씬한 slim

namda, nameun 남다, 남은 left, remaining

namdongjjok 남동쪽 south-east

nameoji 나머지 rest, remainder, leftover

namgida 남기다 leave behind on purpose, to

namhan 남한 South Korea

namja 남자 man

namja chin.gu 남자 친구 boyfriend

(namja) seonggi (남자) 성기 penis

namjjok 남쪽 south

nampyeon 남편 husband

namseojjok 남서쪽 south-west

namseong 남성 male

namu 나무 tree, wood

namuro doen 나무로 된 wooden

N

nancheohada, nancheohan 난처하다, 난처한 embarrassing

nanu.eojida, nanu.eojin 나누어지다, 나누어진 divided by

nanu.eojuda 나누어주다 hand out, to

nanuda 나누다 divide, split up, to

nappeuda, nappeun 나쁘다, 나쁜 bad, wrong (morally)

nara 나라 country (nation)

naseonhyeong(ui) 나선형(의) spiral

nat 낮 day

nat gae(ui) 낱 개(의) loose (not in packet)

nata 낳다 birth, to give

natda, najeun 낮다, 낮은 low

natseon saram 낯선 사람 stranger

ne 네 yes

nektai 넥타이 necktie, tie

neo 너 you (familiar)

neogeureopda, neogeureoun 너그럽다, 너그러운 generous

neohui(deul) 너희(들) you (familiar)

neomeojida 넘어지다 fall over, to

neomgyeojuda 넘겨주다 hand over, to

neomu 너무 too (excessive)

neomu mani 너무 많이 too much

neonsenseu 넌센스 nonsense

neopda, neolbeun 넓다, 넓은 wide, spacious, broad

net 넷 four

neteu 네트 net

neteuwokeu 네트워크 network

neujeodo 늦어도 at the latest

neukkida 느끼다 feel, to

neukkim 느낌 feeling

-neun -는 (present-tense noun-modifying suffix)

-neun/(eu)n che hada -는/(으)ㄴ 체 하다 pretend, to

-neun dong.an -는 동안 while

-neun geot -는 것 act of -ing

-neun jung.e -는 중(에) middle: be in the middle of doing

-neun/(eu)n/(eu)l+(object) -는/(으)ㄴ/(으)ㄹ+ (사물) the object which

-neun/(eu)n/(eu)l+(person) -는/(으)ㄴ/(으)ㄹ+ (사람) the person who

...neun/eun ...는/은 as for, speaking of (topic marker)

-neunde iksukhada -는데 익숙하다 used to, accustomed

-neunde/(eu)nde -는데/(으)ㄴ데 (background information)

neungsukhada, neungsukan 능숙하다, 능숙한 skillful

neurida, neurin 느리다, 느린 slow

neutda, neujeun 늦다, 늦은 late

nim 님 (honorific suffix for addressing)

nochida 놓치다 miss (bus, flight), to

nodong 노동 labor

noe 뇌 brai

nogeum 녹음 tape recording

nokhwahada 녹화하다 videotape, to

nolda 놀다 play, to

nollada, nollawohada 놀라다, 놀라워하다 surprised, astonished

nollapda, nollaun 놀랍다, 놀라운 surprising

non 논 rice fields

o

nongdam 농담 joke
nonggu 농구 basketball
nonjaeng 논쟁 argument
nonjaenghada 논쟁하다 argue, to
nopda, nopeun 높다, 높은 high
nopi 높이 height, level
norae 노래 song
noraehada 노래하다 sing, to
norata, noran 노랗다, 노란 yellow
noryeok 노력 effort
noryeokhada 노력하다 effort, to make an
nota 놓다 place, put, to
nuga 누가 who
nugu 누구 who
nugudeunji 누구든지 anybody, anyone
nun 눈 eye
nun 눈 snow
nuna 누나 older sister (male's)
nuni oda 눈이 오다 snow, to
nunmeolda, nunmeon 눈멀 다, 눈 먼 blind
nunmul 눈물 tears
nunsseop 눈썹 eyebrow
nupda 눕다 lie down, to
nureuda 누르다 press, to
nyujillaendeu 뉴질랜드 New Zealand
nyuseu 뉴스 news

O

o 오 five
obeun 오븐 oven
oda 오다 come, to
odumak 오두막 hut, shack
oechida 외치다 shout, yell, to
oegugin 외국인 foreigner
oeguk(ui) 외국(의) foreign
oemo 외모 appearance, looks
oenjjok 왼쪽 left-hand side

oeropda, oeroun 외롭다, 외 로운 lonely
ohae 오해 misunderstanding
ohu 오후 afternoon
oi 오이 cucumber
ojing.eo 오징어 squid
oksusu 옥수수 sweet corn
olke 올케 sister-in-law
ollida 올리다 raise, lift, increase
ollagada 올라가다 go up, climb, to
olta, oreun 옳다, 옳은 right, correct
omgida 옮기다 move from one place to another, to
omul 오물 dirt, filth
oncheon 온천 hot spring
ondo 온도 temperature
oneul 오늘 today
oneulppam 오늘밤 tonight
oneun gire 오는 길에 on the way
oppa 오빠 older brother (female's)
orae, oraen 오래, 오랜 long (time)
oraedoeda, oraedoen 오래되다, 오래된 old (of things)
oragohada 오라고하다 invite (ask along), to
orenji 오렌지 orange, citrus
orenjisaek(ui) 오렌지 색(의) orange (color)
oreuda 오르다 rise, ascend, to
oreunjjok 오른쪽 right-hand side
ori 오리 duck
oryu 오류 error
osip 오십 fifty
ot 옷 clothes, clothing, garment
ot beotda 옷 벗다 get undressed, to
ot ipda 옷 입다 get dressed, to

O

otgam 옷감 cloth
otobai 오토바이 motorcycle
owol 오월 May
oyeom 오염 pollution

P

pa.eophada 파업하다 strike, to go on
pado 파도 surf, wave (in sea)
paekseu 팩스 fax (machine)
paekseu 팩스 fax (message)
paekseu bonaeda 팩스 보내다 fax, to
paen 팬 fan (admirer)
paenti 팬티 briefs, panties, shorts (underpants)
pagoedoeda, pagoedoen 파괴되다, 파괴된 destroyed
pagoehada 파괴하다 destroy, to
painaepeul 파인애플 pineapple
pajama 파자마 pajamas
pal 팔 arm
pal 팔 eight
palda 팔다 sell, to
paljji 팔찌 bracelet
palkkumchi 팔꿈치 elbow
pallida, pallin 팔리다, 팔린 sold
palsip 팔십 eighty
panjajip 판자집 shack
panji 판지 cardboard
panmae jung 판매 중 sale, for
panmaedae 판매대 stall (of vendor)
panorama 파노라마 panorama
parata, paran 파랗다, 파란 blue
pari 파리 fly (insect)
parwol 팔월 August
pati 파티 party (event)
peiji 페이지 page

peinteu 페인트 paint
pen 펜 pen
peompeu 펌프 pump
peosenteu 퍼센트 percent
peullaseutik 플라스틱 plastic
peulleogeu 플러그 plug (electric)
peulleoseu 플러스 plus
peulluteu 플루트 flute
peurogeuraem 프로그램 program
pi 피 blood
pibu 피부 skin
pigonhada, pigonhan 피곤하다, 피곤한 tired, worn out
pigoyong.in 피고용인 employee
pilleum 필름 film (camera)
pillipin 필리핀 Philippines
pilsu.ida, pilsu(ui) 필수이다, 필수(의) compulsory
pingkeusaek(ui) 핑크색(의) pink
pirohada, pirohan 피로하다, 피로한 weary
piryo 필요 need
piryohada 필요하다 need, to
piryohada, piryohan 필요하다, 필요한 necessary
podo 포도 grapes
podoju 포도주 wine
pohamdoen, pohamhaeseo 포함된, 포함해서 included, including
pohamhada 포함하다 involve, to
pok 폭 width
pokeu 포크 fork
pokpo 폭포 waterfall
pokpung 폭풍 storm
pongnohada 폭로하다 reveal (make known), to
ppalda 빨다 suck, to
ppalgata, ppalgan 빨갛다, 빨간 red
ppalli 빨리 quickly
ppalliyo! 빨리요! hurry up!

ppang 빵 bread
ppareuda, ppareun 빠르다, 빠른 quick, fast, rapid
ppeotppeothada/-han 뻣뻣하다/-한 stiff
...ppunman anira ...do ...뿐만 아니라...도 not only...but also
ppuri 뿌리 root (of plant)
ppyam 뺨 cheek
ppyeo 뼈 bone
pul 풀 grass
pumhaeng.i jota/jo.eun 품행이 좋다/좋은 well-behaved
pureonota 풀어놓다 release, to
pureuda, pureun 푸르다, 푸른 green
pye 폐 lungs
pyeollihada, pyeollihan 편리하다, 편리한 convenient, handy
pyeonanhada/-han 편안하다, 편안한 comfortable
pyeondopyo 편도표 one-way ticket
pyeongbeomhada/-han 평범하다/-한 ordinary
pyeongdeung 평등 equality
pyeonggyun 평균 average (numbers)
pyeonghwa 평화 peace
pyeonghwaropda, pyeonghwaroun 평화롭다/-로운 peaceful
pyeongkkahada 평가하다 estimate, to
pyeongpyeonghada/-han 평평하다/-한 even, flat, smooth, level
pyeongsaeng 평생 lifetime
pyeonji 편지 letter
pyeonji yeollakhada 편지 연락하다 correspond (letters), to
pyo 표 ticket (for transport)

pyohyeonhada 표현하다 express, state, to
pyomyeon 표면 surface
pyosi 표시 sign, symbol

R

radio 라디오 radio
raiteo 라이터 lighter
remon 레몬 lemon, citrus
...reul/eul ...를/을 (object particle)
...reul/eul geochyeoseo ...를/을 거쳐서 via
...reul/eul je.oehago ...를/을 제외하고 except
...reul/eul tonghayeo ...를/을 통하여 through, past, by way of
...reul/eul uisikhada ...를/을 의식하다 conscious of, to be
...reul/eul wihan ...를/을 위한 for
ribon 리본 ribbon

S

sa 사 four
sa bunui il 4 분의 1 quarter
sa.eop 사업 business
sa.eopga 사업가 businessperson
saakhada, saakan 사악하다, 사악한 wicked
sabal 사발 bowl
sabiphada 삽입하다 insert, to
sachal 사찰 temple
sachiseureopda, sachiseureo.un 사치스럽다/-스러운 luxurious
sada 사다 buy, to
sadari 사다리 ladder
sae 새 bird
sae 새 new
sae.u 새우 shrimp, prawn
saebyeok 새벽 dawn
saeda 새다 leak, to

S

saegida 새기다 engrave, to
saehae bok mani badeuseyo!
새해 복 많이 받으세요!
happy new year!
saekkal 색깔 color
saekomdalkomhada/-han
새콤달콤하다/-한
sweet and sour
saelleori 샐러리 celery
saendal 샌달 sandals
saeng.il 생일 birthday
saeng.il chukhahamnida! 생
일 축하합니다! happy
birthday!
saenggak 생각 idea,
thoughts, mind
saenggakhada 생각하다
think, consider, count, reckon
to
saenggang 생강 ginger
saengjwi 생쥐 mouse
(animal)
saengmyeong 생명 life
saengni 생리 period
(menstrual)
saengnihada 생리하다
menstruate, to
saengnyeonworil 생년월일
date of birth
saengsanhada 생산하다
produce, to
saengseon 생선 fish
saeropda, saeroun 새롭다, 새
로운 new
sagikkun 사기꾼 cheat,
someone who cheats
sago 사고 accident
sagwa 사과 apple
sagwahada 사과하다
apologize, to
sagyojeogida/-jeogin 사교적
이다/-적인 friendly, outgoing
sahoe(jeogin) 사회(적인)
social
...saie ...사이에 between
saijeu 사이즈 size
sain 사인 signature

sainhada 사인하다 sign, to
sajang 사장 president, boss,
director (of company)
sajeon 사전 dictionary
sajin 사진 photograph
sajin jjikda 사진 찍다
photograph, to
sajjeogida, sajjeogin 사적이
다, 사적인 private
sakkeon 사건 case (law)
sakkeon 사건 happening,
incident
...sal ...살 years old
salda 살다 live (stay in a
place), to
salmeun 삶은 boiled
sam 삼 three
samak 사막 desert (arid land)
samgakhyeong 삼각형
triangle
samkida 삼키다 swallow, to
samsip 삼십 thirty
samul 사물 object
samusil 사무실 office
samwol 삼월 March
san 산 mountain
sanapda, sanaun 사납다, 사
나운 fierce
sanchaekhada 산책하다 go
for a walk, to
saneop 산업 industry
sang 상 prize
sang.a 상아 ivory
sang.eo 상어 shark
sang.ihada 상의하다
consult, talk over with, to
sangcheo 상처 wound
sangdaebang 상대방
opponent
sangdanghi 상당히 quite,
fairly, rather
sanggisikida 상기시키다
remind, to
sanggwaneopda 상관없다
matter, it doesn't
sanghada, sanghan
상하다, 상한 spoiled (of food)

sanghwang 상황 situation, how things are

sangja 상자 box, chest, crate, case

sangpum 상품 goods

sangsanghada 상상하다 imagine, to

sangtae 상태 condition (status)

sanho 산호 coral

sara itda 살아 있다 alive

sarainneun 살아있는 live (be alive)

saram 사람 person

saramdeul 사람들 people

saranamda 살아남다 survive, to

sarang 사랑 love

saranghada 사랑하다 love, to

sarangseureopda, sarangseureo.un 사랑스럽다/-스러운 lovely

sasil 사실 fact

sasil ida, sasil(ui) 사실이다, 사실(의) true

sasip 사십 forty

sasohada, sasohan 사소하다, 사소한 minor (not important)

satang 사탕 candy, sweets

satangsusu 사탕수수 sugarcane

saturi 사투리 dialect

sawi 사위 son-in-law

sawol 사월 April

sayonghada 사용하다 use, to

...se ...세 years old

se beonjjae 세 번째 third

segi 세기 century

se.gye 세계 world

se.gyun 세균 germ

seil 세일 sale (reduced prices)

seje 세제 detergent

sejuda 세주다 rent out, to

sekseu 섹스 sex, sexual activity

seobeorida 서버리다 stall (car), to

seobiseu 서비스 service

seoda 서다 stand, to

seojjok 서쪽 west

seokda 섞다 mix, to

seokkida, seokkin 섞이다, 섞인 mixed

seolchihada 설치하다 install, to

seolgeojihada 설거지하다 wash the dishes, to

seolliphada 설립하다 establish, set up, to

seolmyeonghada 설명하다 explain, to

seoltang 설탕 sugar

seom 섬 island

seomyeong 서명 signature

seon 선 line (mark)

seon.go 선고 sentence

seoneulhada, seoneulhan 서늘하다, 서늘한 cool

seong 성 surname

seong 성 sex

seongbyeol 성별 gender

seon.geo 선거 election

seon.geum 선금 advance money, deposit

seonggong 성공 success

seonggonghada 성공하다 succeed, to

seongkkyeok 성격 character, personality

seongjanghada 성장하다 grow up (child), to

seongnyang 성냥 matches

seongseureopda, seongseureo.un 성스럽다, 성스러운 sacred

seonhohada 선호하다 prefer, to

seonmul 선물 present, gift

seonmulhada 선물하다 present, to

S

seonsaengnim 선생님 teacher

seonsaengnim 선생님 you (male adult), sir

seontaek 선택 choice

seontaekjeogida, seontaekjeogin 선택적이다/-적인 optional

seontaekhada 선택하다 choose, pick, to

seorap 서랍 drawer

seoreun 서른 thirty

seorikda, seorigeun 설익다, 설익은 rare (uncooked)

seoryu gabang 서류 가방 briefcase

seoyang saram 서양 사람 westerner

set 셋 three

setakso 세탁소 laundry

seteu 세트 set

se.uda 세우다 establish, set up, elect, to

seukejul 스케줄 schedule

seukeurin 스크린 screen (of computer)

seukoteullaendeu 스코틀랜드 Scotland

seullip 슬립 slip (petticoat, underskirt)

seullipeo 슬리퍼 slippers

seulpeuda, seulpeun 슬프다, 슬픈 sad

seulpeum 슬픔 sorrow

seumul 스물 twenty

seunggaek 승객 passenger

seungganggi 승강기 lift, elevator

seupeonji 스펀지 sponge

seupeurei 스프레이 spray

seupocheu 스포츠 sports

seuseuro 스스로 own, on one's

seutaempeu 스탬프 stamp (ink)

seutail 스타일 style

seutobeu 스토브 stove, cooker

seuwichi 스위치 switch

...si ..시 o'clock

si 시 town

siabeoji 시아버지 father-in-law

sibeok 십억 billion

sibi 십이 twelve

sibil 십일 eleven

sibirwol 십일월 November

sibiwol 십이월 December

sibo 십오 fifteen

sicheong 시청 city hall

sida, sin 시다, 신 sour

sido 시도 attempt

sidohada 시도하다 attempt, to

sieomeoni 시어머니 mother-in-law

siga 시가 cigar

sigan 시간 hour

sigan 시간 time

siganeul jal jikida/jikineun 시간을 잘 지키다/ 지키는 punctual

siganpyo 시간표 timetable

sigeumchi 시금치 spinach

sigol 시골 country (rural area)

sigye 시계 clock

sihap 시합 match, game

siheom 시험 exam, test

(siheom) boda (시험) 보다 sit (the test), to

sijak 시작 beginning, starting

sijakhada 시작하다 begin, start, to

sijang 시장 market

sijjeom 시점 point (in time)

sikcho 식초 vinegar

sikdang 식당 restaurant

sikhida 식히다 cool, to

sikkeureopda, sikkeureoun 시끄럽다, 시끄러운 noisy

siksa 식사 meal

siksa junbihada 식사 준비하다 lay the table, to

sil 실 thread

siljikhada, siljikan 실직하다, 실직한 unemployed
siljje(ui) 실제(의) real
siljjero 실제로 actually, really (in fact)
silkeu 실크 silk
sillaebok 실내복 dressing gown
sillang 신랑 bridegroom
sillyehamnida! 실례합니다! excuse me!
silmanghada, silmanghan 실망하다, 실망한 disappointed
silpae 실패 failure
silpaehada 실패하다 fail, to
silssu 실수 mistake
simda 심다 plant, to
simgakhada, simgakan 심각하다, 심각한 serious (not funny)
simhada, simhan 심하다, 심한 severe
simin 시민 citizen
simjang 심장 heart
simman 십만 hundred thousand
simnyuk 십육 sixteen
simsimhada, simsimhan 심심하다, 심심한 bored
sin 신 god
sinae jungsimji 시내 중심지 downtown
sinaegwan.gwang 시내관광 sightseeing
sinbal 신발 shoes
sinbu 신부 bride
sinbu 신부 priest
sincheonghada 신청하다 apply (for permission), to
sincheongseo 신청서 form (application)
singgapol 싱가폴 Singapore
singmul 식물 plant, vegetable
singmurwon 식물원 botanic gardens

sin.gyeong sseuda 신경 쓰다 mind, be displeased, to
sin.gyeong sseuji maseyo! 신경 쓰지 마세요! never mind!
sinhwa 신화 myth
sini nada, sini nan 신이 나다, 신이 난 excited
sinjang 신장 kidney
sinjunghada, sinjunghan 신중하다, 신중한 cautious
sinmun 신문 newspaper
sinnada, sinnaneun 신나다, 신나는 exciting
sinseonghada, sinseonghan 신성하다, 신성한 holy, sacred
sinseonhada, sinseonhan 신선하다, 신선한 fresh
sinu.i 시누이 sister-in-law
sip 십 ten
sip.pal 십팔 eighteen
sipchil 십칠 seventeen
sipdae 십대 teenager
sipgu 십구 nineteen
sipsa 십사 fourteen
sipsam 십삼 thirteen
sireohada 싫어하다 dislike, to
sitda 싣다 load up, to
siteu 시트 sheet (for bed)
siwol 시월 October
so.eum 소음 noise
so.nyeon 소년 boy
sobyeonboda 소변보다 'urinate, to
soegogi 쇠고기 beef
soetoehada 쇠퇴하다 decline (get less), to
sogaehada 소개하다 introduce someone, to
sogeum 소금 salt
sogida 속이다 deceive, cheat, to
sogot 속옷 underwear
sohwabullyang 소화불량 indigestion

S

soilkkeori 소일거리 pastime
sokdo 속도 speed
soketeu 소케트 socket (electric)
sol 솔 brush
soljilhada 솔질하다 brush, to
somaechigi 소매치기 pickpocket
somaechigihada 소매치기하다 pickpocket, to
somun 소문 rumor
son 손 hand
sonagi 소나기 shower (of rain)
sonhae 손해 damage
sonhaeboda 손해보다 lose money, to
sonja 손자 grandson, grandchild
sonjabi 손잡이 handle
sonjeondeung 손전등 flashlight, torch
sonkkarak 손가락 finger
sonmok 손목 wrist
(sonmok)sigye (손목)시계 watch (wristwatch)
sonnim 손님 guest
sonnyeo 손녀 granddaughter, grandchild
sonsangsikida 손상시키다 damage, to
sonsugeon 손수건 handkerchief
sonsure 손수레 cart (pushcart)
sontop 손톱 nail (finger)
sonwi(ui) 손위(의) elder
so.nyeo 소녀 girl
sopa 소파 sofa, couch
sopo 소포 parcel
sori 소리 sound, noise
soriga keuda/keun 소리가 크다/큰 loud
soseol 소설 novel
soseu 소스 sauce
soyuhada 소유하다 possess, own, to

soyumul 소유물 possessions, belongings
ssada 싸다 pack, wrap, to
ssada, ssan 싸다, 싼 cheap, inexpensive
ssal 쌀 rice (uncooked grains)
ssauda 싸우다 fight (physically), to
sseokda, sseogeun 썩다, 썩은 rotten
sseuda 쓰다 spend (money), to
sseuda 쓰다 write (a letter), compose (a poem), note down, to
sseuda, sseun 쓰다, 쓴 bitter
sseulda 쓸다 sweep, to
sseulmo eopda/eomneun 쓸모 없다/없는 useless
sseulmo itda/inneun 쓸모 있다/있는 useful
sseuregi 쓰레기 garbage
ssi 씨 seed
ssidi 씨디 CD
ssidi-rom 씨디롬 CD-ROM
ssipda 씹다 chew, to
ssitda 씻다 wash, to
ssoda 쏘다 shoot, to
su.eop 수업 lesson, class
su.ip 수입 income
su.ip(pum) 수입(품) import
su.iphada 수입하다 import, to
subak 수박 watermelon
suchi 수치 shame, disgrace
suchul(pum) 수출(품) export
suchulhada 수출하다 export, to
sugeon 수건 towel
sugeumhada 수금하다 collect payment, to
sugong.ye 수공예 handicraft
suhaeng 수행 performance
suhaenghada 수행하다 fulfill, to
sujja 숫자 figure, number
sujun 수준 level (standard)

sukgohada 숙고하다
consider, ponder, think over, to
sukkarak 숟가락 spoon
sukso 숙소 accommodation
sul 술 alcohol, liquor
sul chwihada 술 취하다
drunk
suljjip 술집 bar (serving
drinks)
sumda 숨다 hide, to
sumgida 숨기다 hide, to
sumgyeojida, sumgyeojin 숨
겨지다, 숨겨진 hidden
sun.gan 순간 moment
(instant)
sungbaehada 숭배하다
worship, to
sungnyeo 숙녀 lady
sunhada, sunhan 순하다, 순
한 mild (not spicy)
sunjonghada 순종하다 obey,
to
sunjonghada/-haneun 순종하
다/-하는 obedient
sunjoropda, sunjoroun 순조
롭다/순조로운 smooth (to
go smoothly)
suno.eun 수놓은
embroidered
sunseo 순서 order, sequence
sunsuhada, sunsuhan 순수하
다, 순수한 pure
sunwi 순위 ranking
sup 숲 forest
supeomaket 수퍼마켓
supermarket
supyeongseon 수평선
horizon
supyo 수표 cheque
susang 수상 prime minister
susibui 수십의 tens of,
multiples of ten
susuhada, susuhan 수수하다,
수수한 modest, simple
susuryo 수수료 fee
suyeongbok 수영복
swimming costume

suyeonghada 수영하다
bathe, swim, to
suyeongjang 수영장
swimming pool
suyoil 수요일 Wednesday
swida 쉬다 rest, relax, to
swin 쉰 fifty
swipda, swiun 쉽다, 쉬운
simple, easy
syampu 샴푸 shampoo
syawo 샤워 shower (for
washing)
syawohada 샤워하다 take a
shower, to
syeocheu 셔츠 shirt
syo 쇼 show (live performance)
syopeuro 쇼프로 show
(broadcast)
syopinghada 쇼핑하다 shop,
go shopping, to

T

tada 타다 burn, to
tada 타다 get on, board, ride
(transport), to
tae.eonada 태어나다 born,
to be
taedo 태도 attitude
taeguk 태국 Thailand
taeksi 택시 taxi
taepung 태풍 typhoon
tae.uda 태우다 burn, to
taewojuda 태워주다 pick up
(someone), to
taeyang 태양 sun
tago itda 타고 있다 on board
taipinghada 타이핑하다
type, to
tal 탈 mask
tanwonhada 탄원하다
plead, to
tap 탑 tower
tawonhyeong(ui) 타원형(의)
oval (shape)
teibeul 테이블 table
teibeul ppo 테이블 보
tablecloth

T

teipeu 테이프 tape, adhesive

tellebijeon 텔레비전 television

teniseu 테니스 tennis

teok 턱 chin, jaw

teoksuyeom 턱수염 beard

teong bida/bin 텅 비다/빈 empty

teseuteuhada 테스트하다 test, to

teukbyeolhada/-han 특별하다/-한 special

teukhi 특히 particularly, especially

teukjing(jeogin) 특징(적인) characteristic

teullida, teullin 틀리다, 틀린 wrong, mistaken

teullimeopseoyo! 틀림없어요! certainly!

teureok 트럭 truck

tibi 티비 TV

tim 팀 team

tip 팁 tip (gratuity)

tisyeocheu 티셔츠 tee shirt

tochak(ui) 토착 (의) indigenous

toejikhada, toejikan 퇴직하다, 퇴직한 retired

tohada 토하다 vomit, to

tomato 토마토 tomato

tong.yeoksa 통역사 interpreter

tonggwahada 통과하다 pass, go past, to

tonghwa 통화 currency

tonghwajung.ida 통화중이다 busy, engaged (telephone)

tongji 통지 notice

tongjjeung 통증 ache, pain

toyoil 토요일 Saturday

...ttaemune ... 때문에 because of...

ttaerida 때리다 beat, strike, to

ttal 딸 daughter

ttam 땀 sweat

ttam heullida 땀 흘리다 sweat, perspire, to

ttang 땅 ground, earth, land

ttangkong 땅콩 peanut

ttareuda 따르다 obey, to

ttatteutam 따뜻함 warmth

ttatteuthada, ttatteutan 따뜻하다, 따뜻한 warm

tteolda 떨다 shake, shiver, to

tteonada 떠나다 leave, depart, to

tteoreojida 떨어지다 fall, drop, to

tteoreojida 떨어지다 finished (none left)

tteoreojyeoseo 떨어져서 apart

tteoreotteurida 떨어뜨리다 drop, to

tto bopsida! 또 봅시다! see you later!

ttohan 또한 too (also)

ttokbareuda, ttokbareun 똑바르다, 똑바른 straight

ttokbaro 똑바로 straight ahead

ttokttokhada, ttokttokan 똑똑하다, 똑똑한 smart

ttoneun 또는 or

ttong 똥 shit

ttukkeong 뚜껑 lid

ttulta 뚫다 pierce, penetrate, to

ttungttunghada/-han 뚱뚱하다/-한 fat, plump, stout

tupyohada 투표하다 vote, to

tusu 투수 pitcher

twi.eonaoda 튀어나오다 stick out, to

twigida 튀기다 fry, to

twigin 튀긴 fried

U

uahada, uahan 우아하다, 우아한 elegant

ucheguk 우체국 post office

...ui ...의 (possessive particle)

...ui bakkate ...의 바깥에 outside of...

uido 의도 intention

uigyeon 의견 opinion

uihak(ui) 의학(의) medical

uija 의자 chair

uimi 의미 meaning

uimihada 의미하다 mean (word), to

uinon 의논 discussion

uinonhada 의논하다 discuss, to

uisa 의사 doctor

uisimhada 의심하다 doubt, suspect, to

ul 울 wool

ulda 울다 cry, weep, to

ullida 울리다 ring (bell), to

ultari 울타리 fence

umjigiji anta/anneun 움직이지 않다/않는 stuck, won't move

umul 우물 well (for water)

un 운 luck

un jota/jo.eun 운 좋다/좋은 lucky

uni eopda/eomneun 운이 없다/없는 unlucky

unjeonhada 운전하다 drive (a car), to

upyeonmul 우편물 mail, post

upyo 우표 stamp (postage)

uri 우리 we, us

uri(ui) 우리(의) our

usan 우산 umbrella

useungja 우승자 winner

usuhada, usuhan 우수하다, 우수한 excellent

utda 웃다 laugh, to

utgida, utgineun 웃기다, 웃기는 humorous

uyeonhi 우연히 accidentally, by chance

uyu 우유 milk

W

...wa/gwa ...와/과 and

...wa/gwa bigyohaeseo ...와/과 비교해서 compared with

waeyo? 왜요? why?

wakseu 왁스 wax

wanbyeokhada, wanbyeokan 완벽하다/-한 perfect

wandukong 완두콩 peas, green beans

wang 왕 king

wangbokpyo 왕복표 return ticket

wanjeonhada, wanjeonhan 완전하다/-한 whole, complete

wanjeonhi 완전히 completely

wanseonghada 완성하다 complete, to

wepsaiteu 웹사이트 website

wicheung 위층 upstairs

wichihada 위치하다 be located, be situated, to

...wie ...위에 above, upstairs

...wie ...위에 on, at

...wie ...위에 up, upward

...wihae goandoeda ...위해 고안되다 intended for

wiheom 위험 danger

wiheomhada, wiheomhan 위험하다, 위험한 dangerous

wihyeophada 위협하다 threaten, to

...wiro ...위로 up, upward

won 원 circle

wonbon 원본 original

wonhada 원하다 want, to

wonin 원인 cause

wonsung.i 원숭이 ape, monkey

woryoil 월요일 Monday

Y Y

yachae 야채 greens, vegetables
yagan 야간 nightly
yagu 야구 baseball
yak 약 approximately, around
yak 약 drug, medicine
yakgan 약간 bit, slightly
yakgan(ui) 약간(의) some
yakganui 약간의 mild, slight (not severe)
yakguk 약국 drugstore, pharmacy
yakhada, yakan 약하다, 약한 weak
yakhonhada/-han 약혼하다/-한 engaged (to be married)
yakhonja 약혼자 fiancé
yakhonnyeo 약혼녀 fiancée
yaksok 약속 appointment
yaksokhada 약속하다 promise, to
yang 양 amount
yang 양 sheep
yang.yukhada 양육하다 raise, bring up (children), to
yangbaechu 양배추 cabbage
yangcho 양초 candle
yangdong.i 양동이 bucket
yanggogi 양고기 lamb, mutton
yangmal 양말 socks
yangmo 양모 wool
yangnyeom 양념 spices
yangpa 양파 onion
yasaeng 야생 wild
yatda, yateun 얕다, 얕은 shallow
ye 예 example
ye 예 ye
yebang jeopjong 예방 접종 vaccination
yegeumhada 예금하다 deposit (put money in the bank), to
yego 예고 notice

yei 예의 manners
ye.ibareuda, ye.ibareun 예의바르다/-바른 well-mannered
yejeol 예절 manners
yennal 옛날 in olden times
yeoboseyo! 여보세요! hello! (on phone)
yeodeol 여덟 eight
yeodeun 여든 eighty
yeogi 여기 here
yeogwan 여관 guesthouse, lodge, small hotel
yeohaeng 여행 trip, journey
yeohaeng jal danyeo.oseyo! 여행 잘 다녀오세요! bon voyage!
yeohaenggabang 여행가방 luggage, suitcase
yeohaenghada 여행하다 travel, to
yeohaengja 여행자 traveler
yeoja 여자 woman
(yeoja) seonggi (여자) 성기 vagina
yeojachin.gu 여자 친구 girlfriend
yeok 역 train station
yeokgyeopda, yeokgyeo.un 역겹다, 역겨운 disgusting
yeokhal 역할 role
yeokkwon 여권 passport
yeoksa 역사 history
yeoksi 역시 also
yeol 열 fever
yeol 열 ten
yeolda 열다 open, to
yeoldaseot 열다섯 fifteen
yeolhana 열하나 eleven
yeollak 연락 contact, connection
yeollakhada 연락하다 contact, get in touch with, to
yeollida, yeollin 열리다, 열린 open
yeolnet 열넷 fourteen
yeolset 열셋 thirteen

yeolsoe 열쇠 key (to room)
yeolttul 열둘 twelve
yeolyeodeol 열여덟 eighteen
yeolyeoseot 열여섯 sixteen
yeomso 염소 goat
yeon 년 year
yeon.gan 연간 annual
yeon.gi 연기 smoke
yeon.gidoeda, yeon.gidoen 연기되다, 연기된 postponed
yeon.gihada 연기하다 delay, postpone, put off, to
yeon.gyeolhada 연결하다 connect/join together, to
yeong 영 zero
yeong.eo 영어 English
yeong.wonhi 영원히 forever
yeonggujeogida, yeonggujeogin 영구적이다 /-적인 permanent
yeongguk 영국 England
yeongguk(ui) 영국(의) British
yeonghwa 영화 film, movie
yeonghwagwan 영화관 movie house, cinema
yeonghyang 영향 influence
yeonghyang.eul juda 영향을 주다 affect, influence, to
yeon.gi 연기 performance
yeongnihada, yeongnihan 영리하다, 영리한 clever
yeongsujeung 영수증 receipt
yeon.gu 연구 research
yeon.guhada 연구하다 research, to
yeonhoe 연회 banquet
yeonjangja 연장자 elder
yeonpil 연필 pencil
yeonseol 연설 speech
yeonseolhada 연설하다 speech, to make a
yeonseup 연습 practice
yeonseuphada 연습하다 practice, to

...yeope ...옆에 next to, beside
yeopseo 엽서 postcard
yeorahop 열아홉 nineteen
yeoreo 여러 several
yeoreobun 여러분 you (audience)
yeoreum 여름 summer
yeorilgop 열일곱 seventeen
yeoseong 여성 female
yeoseot 여섯 six
yeosin 여신 goddess
yeowang 여왕 queen
yeppeuda, yeppeun 예쁘다, 예쁜 beautiful, pretty
yereul deuljamyeon 예를 들 자면 such as, for example
(ye)sik (예)식 ceremony
yesul 예술 art
yesulga 예술가 artist
yesun 예순 sixty
yeyak 예약 reservation
yeyakhada 예약하다 reserve, ask for in advance, to
...yeyo/ieyo ...예요/이에요 be (copula, polite ending)
yocheonghada 요청하다 request (formally), to
yogeum 요금 fare, rate, tariff
yoguhada 요구하다 claim, demand, to
yoil 요일 day of the week
yojeum 요즘 presently, nowadays
yonggamhada/-han 용감하 다, 용감한 brave, daring
yongmang 욕망 desire
yongseohada 용서하다 forgive, to
yongsucheol 용수철 spring (metal part)
yori 요리 cooking, cuisine, dish
yoriga doeda/doen 요리가 되다/된 cooked
yorihada 요리하다 cook, to
yorisa 요리사 cook (person)

yosae 요새 fortress
yoso 요소 element
youngseo 용서 forgiveness, mercy
yoyak 요약 outline
yuchanghada, yuchanghan 유창하다, 유창한 fluent
yugamida 유감이다 afraid
yugamseureopda 유감스럽다 regret, to
yugamseureopda/-seureo.un 유감스럽다/-스러운 sorry, regretful
yugamseureopgedo 유감스럽게도 regrettably
yugyo 유교 Confucianism
yuhyohada, yuhyohan 유효하다, 유효한 valid

yu.ilhan 유일한 sole, only
yujoe.ida, yujoe.in 유죄이다, 유죄인 guilty (of a crime)
yuk 육 six
yukgun 육군 army
yuksip 육십 sixty
yumul 유물 remains (historical)
yumyeonghada, yumyeonghan 유명하다, 유명한 famous
yuraehada 유래하다 originate, come from, to
yureop 유럽 Europe
yuri 유리 glass (material)
yuryeong 유령 ghost
yuwol 유월 June

English–Korean

A

abdomen bae 배
able to -(eu)l su itda -(으)ㄹ 수 있다
about (approximately) ...jeongdo ...정도
about (regarding) ...e daehae ...에 대해
above, upstairs ...wie ...위 에
abroad hae.oe.e(seo) 해외 에(서)
absent gyeolseokhada, gyeolseokan 결석하다, 결 석한
accept, to batda, badadeurida 받다, 받아들이다
accident sago 사고
accidentally, by chance uyeonhi 우연히
accommodation sukso 숙소
accompany, to gachi gada 같이 가다
according to ...e uihamyeon ...에 의하면
accuse, to binanhada, gosohada 비난하다, 고소하 다
ache tongjjeung 통증
ache, to apeuda 아프다
acquaintance aneun saram 아는 사람
acquainted, to be alda, iksukhada 알다, 익숙하다
across geonneoseo 건너서
across from geonneopyeone 건너편에
act, to haenghada 행하다
action haengdong 행동
activity hwalttong 활동
actually siljjero 실제로

add, to deohada 더하다
address juso 주소
admire, to gamtanhada 감탄 하다
admit, confess, to injeonghada 인정하다
adult eoreun 어른
advance, go forward, to apeuro naagada 앞으로 나 아가다
advance money, deposit seon.geum 선금
advice chunggo 충고
advise, to chunggohada 충고 하다
aeroplane bihaenggi 비행기
affect, to yeonghyang.eul juda 영향을 주다
affection aejeong 애정
afford, to -(eu)l yeoyuga itda -(으)ㄹ 여유가 있다
afraid museowohada, yugamida 무서워하다, 유감 이다
after ...dwie, ...hue **(place)** 뒤에, **(time)** 후에
afternoon ohu 오후
afterwards, then geu hue 그 후에
again dasi 다시
age nai 나이
ago ...jeone ...전에
agree, to dong.ihada 동의하 다
agree to do something, to -giro hada -기로 하다
agreed! chanseong! 찬성!
agreement dong.i 동의
air gonggi 공기
air conditioning naengnanbang 냉난방

A

airmail hanggong.upyeon 항
공우편

airplane bihanggi 비행기

airport gonghang 공항

alcohol, liquor sul 술

alike gatda, gachi 같다, 같이

a little jogeum 조금

alive sara itda 살아 있다

all modeun, modu 모든, 모두

alley, lane golmokgil 골목길

allow, permit, to heorakhada
허락하다

allowed to -a/eodo jota -아/
어도 좋다

almost geo.i 거의

alone honjaitda, honja(seo)
혼자 있다, 혼자(서)

a lot manta, mani
많다, 많이

already beolsseo 벌써

also yeoksi 역시

although birok -jiman/-
(eu)ljirado 비록 -지만/-(으)ㄹ
지라도

altogether, in total modu 모
두

always hangsang 항상

ambassador daesa 대사

America miguk 미국

American miguk saram 미국
사람

among ...jung.e(seo) ...중에
(서)

amount yang, geumaek 양,
금액

ancestor josang 조상

ancient godae(ui) 고대(의)

and geurigo, ...gwa/wa 그리
고, ...과/와

anger hwa 화

angry hwanada, hwanan 화
나다, 화난

animal dongmul 동물

ankle balmok 발목

annoyed jjajeung.i nada 짜증
이 나다

annual yeon.gan 연간

another (different) dareun
다른

another (same again) hana
deo 하나 더

answer, response (spoken)
daedap 대답

answer, response (written)
dapjang 답장

answer, respond, to
daedaphada 대답하다

answer, respond (written), to
dapjanghada 답장하다

answer the phone, to
jeonhwa batda 전화 받다

answering machine
jadong eungdapgi
자동 응답기

antiques golttongpum 골동
품

anus hangmun 항문

anybody, anyone nugudeunji
누구든지

anything mueosideunji 무엇
이든지

anywhere eodideunji 어디
든지

apart tteoreojyeoseo 떨어
져서

apartment apateu 아파트

ape wonsung.i 원숭이

apologize, to sagwahada 사
과하다

apparently myeongbaekhi 명
백히

appear, become visible, to
boida 보이다

appearance, looks oemo 외
모

apple sagwa 사과

appliance, electrical jeonja
jepum 전자 제품

apply (for permission), to
sincheonghada 신청하다

appointment yaksok,
immyeong 약속, 임명

approach (in space), to
jeopgeunhada 접근하다

approach (in time), to
gakkawojida 가까워지다
appropriate jeokdanghada,
jeokdanghan 적당하다, 적당한
approximately yak 약
April sawol 사월
architecture geonchuk 건축
area jiyeok 지역
argue, to nonjaenghada 논쟁
하다
argument nonjaeng 논쟁
arm pal 팔
armchair allak uija 안락 의자
army yukgun 육군
around (approximately) yak
약
around (nearby) ...gakkaie
...가까이에
around (surrounding) ...juwie
...주위에
arrange, to junbihada 준비
하다
arrangements, planning
junbi 준비
arrival dochak 도착
arrive, to dochakhada 도착하
다
art yesul 예술
article (in newspaper) gisa
기사
artificial in.gongjeogida,
in.gongjeogin 인공적이다/-
적인
artist yesulga 예술가
ashamed bukkeureopda,
bukkeureowohada 부끄럽다
/부끄러워하다
Asia asia 아시아
ask about, to ...e daehae
mureoboda ...에 대해 물어
보다
ask for, request, to butakhada
부탁하다
asleep jago itda 자고 있다
assemble, gather, to
mo.euda, moida 모으다, 모
이다

assemble, put together, to
joriphada 조립하다
assist, to dopda 돕다
assistance doum 도움
astonished nollada 놀라다
as well ...do ttohan ...도 또
한
at ...e(seo) ...에(서)
at home (feel) ma.eum
pyeonhada 마음 편하다
atmosphere, ambience
bunwigi 분위기
at night bame 밤에
at once got 곧
attack (in war) gonggyeok
공격
attack (with words) binan
비난
attain, reach, to
dalseonghada 달성하다
attempt sido 시도
attempt, to sidohada 시도
하다
attend, to chamseokhada 참
석하다
at the latest neujeodo 늦어
도
attitude taedo 태도
attractive maeryeokjeogida,
maeryeokjeogin 매력적이다
/-적인
aubergine, eggplant gaji 가지
auction, to gyeongmaehada
경매하다
auctioned off gyeongmaero
pallida 경매로 팔리다
August parwol 팔월
aunt ajumeoni 아주머니
Australia hoju 호주
Australian hoju saram 호주
사람
authority (person in charge)
damdanggwan 담당관
authority (power) gwonhan
권한
automobile, car jadongcha
자동차

autumn ga.eul 가을
available itda 있다 (time, material, person)
available, to make itge hada 있게 하다 (time, material, person)
average (numbers) pyeonggyun 평균
average (so-so) botong.ida, botong.ui 보통이다, 보통(의)
awake kkae.eo itda 깨어 있다
awake, wake up, to kkae.eo nada 깨어나다
awaken, wake someone up, to kkae.uda 깨우다
aware insikhada 인식하다
awareness insik 인식

B

baby agi 아기
back (part of body) deung 등
back, rear dwi 뒤
back, to go doragada 돌아가다
back up, to dwiro gada 뒤로 가다
backward dwiro 뒤로
bad nappeuda, nappeun 나쁘다, 나쁜
bad luck burun 불운
bag gabang 가방
baggage jim 짐
bake, to gupda 굽다
baked guun 구운
bald daemeorida, daemeoriin 대머리이다, 대머리인
ball gong 공
ball point bolpen 볼펜
banana banana 바나나
bandage bungdae 붕대
bank (finance) eunhaeng 은행
bank (of river) duk 둑
banquet yeonhoe 연회
bar (blocking way) chadanbong 차단봉

bar (serving drinks) suljjip 술집
barber ibalsa 이발사
barely gyeo.u 겨우
bargain, to heungjeonghada 흥정하다
barren memareun 메마른
base, foundation gicho 기초
baseball yagu 야구
based on ...e gichohada/ han ...에 기초하다/기초한
basic gibonjeogida, gibonjeogin 기본적이다, 기본적인
basis geun.geo 근거
basket baguni 바구니
basketball nonggu 농구
bath mogyok 목욕
bathe, take a bath, to mogyokhada 목욕하다
bathe, swim, to suyeonghada 수영하다
bathrobe mogyokgaun 목욕가운
bathroom hwajangsil, mogyoksil 화장실, 목욕실
battle jeontu 전투
bay man 만
be, exist, to itda 있다
beach badatga 바닷가
bean kong 콩
bean curd dubu 두부
beard teoksuyeom 턱수염
beat (to defeat), to igida 이기다
beat (to strike), to ttaerida 때리다
beautiful (of people) yeppeuda, yeppeun 예쁘다, 예쁜
beautiful (of places) areumdapda, areumdaun 아름답다/-다운
beautiful (of things) meotjida, meotjin 멋지다, 멋진
because -gi ttaemune -기 때문에

become, to doeda 되다
bed chimdae 침대
bedding, bedclothes chimgu 침구
bedroom chimsil 침실
bedsheet chimdaesiteu 침대 시트
beef soegogi 쇠고기
beer maekju 맥주
before (in front of) ape 앞에
before (in time) jeone 전에
beforehand miri 미리
begin, to sijakhada 시작하다
beginning sijak 시작
behave, to cheosinhada 처신하다
behind dwie 뒤에
belief, faith mideum 믿음
believe, to mitda 믿다
belongings soyumul 소유물
belong to ...e sokada ...에 속하다
below, downstairs arae.e 아래에
belt belteu 벨트
beside yeope 옆에
besides gedaga 게다가
best jeil jota/jo.eun 제일 좋다/좋은
best wishes jal doegireul barada 잘 되기를 바라다
better deo jota/jo.eun 더 좋다/좋은
better, get (be cured), to hoebokdoeda 회복되다
better, get (improve), to joajida 좋아지다
between ...saie ...사이에
bicycle jajeon.geo 자전거
big keuda, keun 크다, 큰
bill gyesanseo 계산서
billion sibeok 십억
bird sae 새
birth, to give nata 낳다
birthday saeng.il 생일
biscuit biseuket, gwaja 비스켓, 과자

bit (part) jogeum 조금
bit (slightly) yakgan 약간
bite, to mulda 물다
bitter sseuda, sseun 쓰다, 쓴
black kkamata, kkaman 까맣다, 까만
black beans kkaman kong 까만 콩
blame, to binanhada 비난하다
bland mumigeonjohada/-han 무미건조하다/-한
blanket damnyo 담요
blind nunmeolda, nunmeon 눈멀다, 눈 먼
blood pi 피
blouse beullauseu 블라우스
blue parata, paran 파랗다, 파란
board (bus, train), to tada 타다
boat bae 배
body mom 몸
boil, to kkeurida 끓이다
boiled kkeurin, salmeun 끓인, 삶은
bone ppyeo 뼈
bon voyage! yeohaeng jal danyeo.oseyo! 여행 잘 다녀오세요!
book chaek 책
border (between countries) gyeonggye 경계
border, edge gajangjari 가장자리
bored simsimhada 심심하다
boring jiruhada, jiruhan 지루하다, 지루한
born, to be tae.eonada 태어나다
borrow, to billida 빌리다
boss sajang, boseu 사장, 보스
botanic gardens singmurwon 식물원
both dul da 둘 다
both...and ...do ...do ...도 ...도

B

bother, disturb, to
banghaehada 방해하다
bother, disturbance banghae
방해
bottle byeong 병
bottom (base) gicho 기초
bottom (buttocks)
eongdeong.i 엉덩이
boundary, border gyeonggye
경계
bowl sabal 사발
box sangja 상자
box (cardboard) sangja 상자
boy so.nyeon 소년
boyfriend namja chin.gu 남
자 친구
bra beuraejieo 브래지어
bracelet paljji 팔찌
brain noe 뇌
brake beureikeu 브레이크
brake, to beureikeu bapda
브레이크 밟다
branch jijeom, gaji 지점, 가지
brave, daring yonggamhada /-
han 용감하다, 용감한
bread ppang 빵
break, shatter, to
kkaetteurida 깨뜨리다
break apart, to jjogaeda 쪼
개다
break down (car, machine),
to gojangnada 고장나다
breakfast, morning meal
achim siksa 아침 식사
breakfast, to eat achim
siksahada 아침 식사하다
breasts gaseum 가슴
bride sinbu 신부
bridegroom sillang 신랑
bridge dari 다리
brief gandanhada, gandanhan
간단하다, 간단한
briefcase seoryu gabang 서
류 가방
briefs paenti 팬티
bright bakda, balgeun 밝다,
밝은

bring, to gajyeo.oda 가져
오다
bring up (children), to
yangnyukhada 양육하다
bring up (topic), to
georonhada 거론하다
British yeongguk(ui) 영국(의)
broad, spacious neopda,
neolbeun 넓다, 넓은
broadcast, program
bangsong 방송
broadcast, to bangsonghada
방송하다
broccoli beurokeolli 브로콜리
broken (of bones, etc.)
bureojida, bureojin 부러지다,
부러진
broken, does not work
gojangnada, gojangnan 고장
나다/-난
broken, shattered kkaejida,
kkaejin 깨지다, 깨진
broken off bureojyeo nagada
부러져나가다
bronze cheongdong 청동
broom bijjaru 빗자루
broth, soup guk 국
brother hyeongje 형제
brother-in-law cheonam,
hyeongbu, maeje 처남, 형부,
매제
brown galsaek(ui) 갈색(의)
bruise meong 멍
brush sol, but 솔, 붓
brush, to soljilhada 솔질하다
bucket yangdong.i 양동이
Buddhism bulgyo 불교
Buddhist bulgyosinja 불교신자
buffalo (water buffalo)
mulso 물소
build, to jitda 짓다
building bilding 빌딩
burglar gangdo, doduk 강도,
도둑
burn (injury) hwasang 화상
burn, to tae.uda, tada 태우
다, 타다

burned down, out da tada
다 타다
bury mutda 묻다
bus beoseu 버스
bus station beoseu
jeonggeojang 버스 정거장
business sa.eop 사업
businessperson sa.eopga 사
업가
busy (crowded) bokjaphada,
bokjapan 복잡하다, 복잡한
busy (doing something)
bappeuda, bappeun 바쁘다,
바쁜
busy (telephone)
tonghwajung.ida 통화중이다
but geureona, -jiman 그러나,
-지만
butter beoteo 버터
butterfly nabi 나비
buttocks eongdeong.i 엉덩이
button danchu 단추
buy, to sada 사다
by (author, artist) ...e uihae
...에 의해
by means of ...(eu)ro ...(으)로
by the way geureonde 그런
데

C

cabbage yangbaechu 양배추
cabbage, Chinese baechu 배
추
cake, pastry keikeu 케이크
calculate, to gyesanhada 계
산하다
calculator gyesan.gi 계산기
call, summon, to bureuda 부
르다
call on the telephone, to
jeonhwahada 전화하다
called, named bullida,
bullineun 불리다, 불리는
calm goyohada, goyohan 고
요하다, 고요한
Cambodia kambodia 캄보
디아

camera kamera 카메라
can, be able to -(eu)l su itda
-(으)ㄹ 수 있다
can, may -a /eodo jota -아/ 어
도 좋다
can, tin kkangtong 깡통
cancel, to chwisohada 취소
하다
candle yangcho 양초
candy, sweets satang 사탕
can't mot 못
cap moja 모자
capable of, to be -(eu)l su
itda -(으)ㄹ 수 있다
capture, to japda 잡다
car, automobile jadongcha
자동차
cardboard panji 판지
cards, game kadeu(nori) 카
드(놀이)
care for, love, to joahada 좋
아하다
care of, to take dolboda 돌
보다
careful! josimhaseyo! 조심
하세요!
career gyeongryeok 경력
carpet kapeteu 카페트
carrot danggeun 당근
carry, to gajyeo.oda,
gajyeogada 가져오다, 가져
가다
cart (pushcart) sonsure 손
수레
cartoon manhwa 만화
carve, to jogakhada 조각하다
carving jogak 조각
case sangja, sakkeon,
gyeong.u 상자, 사건, 경우
cash, money hyeon.geum
현금
cash a check, to
hyeon.geumeuro bakkuda
현금으로 바꾸다
cassette kaseteu 카세트
cat goyang.i 고양이
catch, to japda 잡다

C

cauliflower keollipeullawo 컬리플라워
cause wonin 원인
cautious sinjunghada, sinjunghan 신중하다, 신중한
cave donggul 동굴
CD ssidi 씨 디
CD-ROM ssidi-rom 씨 다롬
ceiling cheonjang 천장
celebrate, to chukhahada 축하하다
celery saelleori 샐러리
cell phone haendeupon 핸드폰
center (of city) jungsimji 중심지
center, middle jung.ang, jungsim 중앙, 중심
central jung.ang(ui), jungsim(ui) 중앙(의), 중심(의)
century segi 세기
ceremony (ye)sik (예)식
certain, sure hwaksilhada, hwaksilhan 확실하다, 확실한
certainly! teullimeopseoyo! 틀림없어요!
certificate jeungmyeongseo 증명서
chair uija 의자
challenge dojeon 도전
champion chaempi.eon 챔피언
chance, by uyeonhi 우연히
chance, opportunity gihoe 기회
change, small jandon 잔돈
change, to (conditions, situations) bakkuda 바꾸다
change, exchange (money), to hwanjeonhada 환전하다
change, switch (clothes), to garaipda 갈아입다
change one's mind, to ma.eumeul bakkuda 마음을 바꾸다
character (personality) seongkkyeok 성격

character (written) geuljja 글자
characteristic teukjing(jeogin) 특징(적인)
chase, to jjotda 쫓다
chase away, chase out, to jjochanaeda 쫓아내다
cheap ssada, ssan 싸다, 싼
cheat, someone who cheats sagikkun 사기꾼
cheat, to sogida 속이다
check, verify, to chekeuhada 체크하다
checked (pattern) chekeumunui 체크무늬
cheek ppyam 뺨
cheers! geonbae! 건배!
cheese chijeu 치즈
cheque supyo 수표
chess cheseu 체스
chest (box) sangja 상자
chest (breast) gaseum 가슴
chew, to ssipda 씹다
chicken dak 닭
chicken meat dakgogi 닭고기
child (offspring) ai 아이
child (young person) eorini 어린이
chilli paste gochujang 고추장
chilli pepper gochu 고추
chilled naengjanghada, naengjanghan 냉장하다, 냉장한
chin teok 턱
China jungguk 중국
Chinese jungguk saram, junggugeo 중국 사람, 중국어
chocolate chokollet 초콜렛
choice seontaek 선택
choose, to seontaekhada 선택하다
chopsticks jeotgarak 젓가락
Christian gidokgyosinja 기독교신자

58

C

ENGLISH–KOREAN

Christianity gidokgyo 기독교
church gyohoe 교회
cigar siga 시가
cigarette dambae 담배
cinema yeonghwagwan 영화관
circle won 원
citizen simin 시민
citrus gamgyullyu 감귤류
city dosi 도시
claim, to yoguhada 요구하다
clap, to baksuchida 박수치다
class, category gyegeup 계급
classes (at university) gang.ui, su.eop 강의, 수업
clean kkaekkeuthada, kkaekkeutan 깨끗하다, 깨끗한
clean, to cheongsohada 청소하다
cleanliness cheonggyeol 청결
clear (of weather) makda, malgeun 맑다, 맑은
clever yeongnihada, yeongnihan 영리하다, 영리한
climate gihu 기후
climb onto, into, to ipda 입다
climb up (hills, mountains), to ...e oreuda ...에 오르다
clock sigye 시계
close, cover, to deopda, datda 덮다, 닫다
close to, nearby ..(e) gakkaun/gakkai ..(에) 가까운/가까이
close together chinhada, chinhan 친하다, 친한
closed (door) dachida, dachin 닫히다, 닫힌
closed (road) makhida, makin 막히다, 막힌
closed (shop) kkeunnada, kkeunnan 끝나다, 끝난
cloth otgam 옷감

clothes, clothing ot 옷
cloudy, overcast heurida, heurin 흐리다, 흐린
clown gwangdae 광대
coat, jacket jaket 자켓
coat, overcoat koteu 코트
coconut kokoneot 코코넛
coffee keopi 커피
coin dongjeon 동전
cold chupda, chuun 춥다, 추운
cold, flu gamgi 감기
colleague, co-worker dongnyo 동료
collect payment, to sugeumhada 수금하다
collide, to chungdolhada 충돌하다
collision chungdol 충돌
color saekkal 색깔
comb bit 빗
come, to oda 오다
come back, to doraoda 돌아오다
come in , to deureo.oda 들어오다
come on!, let's go! eoseoyo! 어서요!
comfortable pyeonanhada, pyeonanhan 편안하다, 편안한
command, order myeongnyeong 명령
command, to myeongnyeonghada 명령하다
common, frequent heunhada, heunhan 흔하다, 흔한
company, firm hoesa 회사
compare, to bigyohada 비교하다
compared with ...gwa/wa bigyohaeseo ...과/와 비교해서
compete, to gyeongjaenghada 경쟁하다
competition gyeongjaeng 경쟁

C

complain, to bulpyeonghada
불평하다
complaint bulpyeong 불평
complete (finished)
kkeunnada, kkeunnan 끝나
다, 끝난
complete (thorough)
cheoljjohada, cheoljeohan 철
저하다/-한
complete (whole)
wanjeonhada, wanjeonhan
완전하다, 완전한
complete, to wanseonghada,
kkeunnaeda 완성하다, 끝내다
completely wanjeonhi 완전
히
complicated bokjaphada,
bokjapan 복잡하다, 복잡한
compose (books, music), to
sseuda, jakgokhada 쓰다, 작
곡하다
composition, writings
jangmun, jakgok 작문, 작곡
compulsory pilsu.ida, pilsu(ui)
필수이다, 필수(의)
computer keompyuteo 컴퓨
터
concentrate, to jipjunghada
집중하다
concerning ...e daehae ...에
대해
condition (pre-condition)
jokkeon 조건
condition (status) sangtae
상태
confectionery gwaja 과자
confidence jasin 자신
confidence, to have jasin itda
자신 있다
Confucianism yugyo 유교
confuse, to hollansikida,
hondongsikida 혼란/ 혼동시
키다
confused (in a mess)
hollanseureopda 혼란스럽다
confused (mentally)
hondonghada 혼동하다

confusing hollansikineun,
hondongsikineun 흔란/혼동
시키는
congratulations!
chukhahaeyo! 축하해요!
connect together, to
yeon.gyeolhada 연결하다
conscious of, to be ...eul /reul
uisikhada ...을/를 의식하다
consider (to have an
opinion), to saenggakhada
생각하다
consider (to think over), to
sukgohada 숙고하다
consult, talk over with, to
sang.ihada 상의하다
contact, connection yeollak
연락
contact, get in touch with, to
yeollakhada 연락하다
continent daeryuk 대륙
continue, to gyesokhada 계
속하다
convenient pyeollihada,
pyeollihan 편리하다, 편리한
conversation daehwa
대화
cook (person) yorisa 요리사
cook, to yorihada 요리하다
cooked yoriga doeda/doen
요리가 되다/된
cooker, stove seutobeu 스토
브
cookie, sweet biscuit kuki
쿠키
cooking, cuisine yori 요리
cool seoneulhada, seoneulhan
서늘하다, 서늘한
cool, to sikhida 식히다
copper guri 구리
copy boksa 복사
coral sanho 산호
corn, grain gongmul 곡물
corner koneo 코너
correct matda, manneun 맞
다, 맞는
correct, to gochida 고치다

correspond (letters), to
pyeonji yeollakhada 편지 연
락하다
corridor bokdo 복도
cost (expense) biyong 비용
cost (price) gap 값
cotton myeon 면
couch, sofa sopa 소파
cough gichim 기침
cough, to gichimhada 기침
하다
could, might -(eu)l sudo itda
-(으)ㄹ 수도 있다
count, reckon, to
saenggakhada 생각하다
counter (for paying,
buying tickets) kaunteu
카운트
country (nation) nara
나라
country (rural area) sigol
시골
courgettes, zucchini
(ae)hobak (애)호박
courtyard madang 마당
cover, to deopda 덮다
cow amso 암소
co-worker, colleague
dongnyo 동료
crab ge 게
cracked geumi gada/gan 금
이 가다/간
cracker, salty biscuit
keuraekeo 크래커
crafts gong.ye 공예
crafts person gong.yega 공
예가
crate sangja 상자
crazy michida, michin 미치
다, 미친
create, to changjohada 창조
하다
criminal beomin 범인
cross, angry hwanada,
hwanan 화나다, 화난
cross, go over, to geonneoda
건너다

crowded bumbida,
bumbineun 붐비다, 붐비는
cruel janinhada, janinhan 잔
인하다, 잔인한
cry, to ulda 울다
cry out, to bureujitda 부르
짖다
cucumber oi 오이
cuisine, style of cooking yori
요리
culture munhwa 문화
cup keop 컵
cupboard chanjang 찬장
cure (medical) chiryo 치료
cured, preserved
jeojangdoeda, jeojangdoen
저장되다, 저장된
currency tonghwa 통화
curtain keoteun 커튼
custom, tradition gwanseup
관습
cut, slice jogak 조각
cut, to jareuda 자르다
cute gwiyeopda, gwiyeo.un
귀엽다, 귀여운

D

daily ilgan, haru.ui 일간, 하
루의
damage sonhae 손해
damage, to sonsangsikida 손
상시키다
damp chukchukhada,
chukchukan 축축하다, 축
축한
dance chum 춤
dance, to chumchuda 춤추다
danger wiheom 위험
dangerous wiheomhada,
wiheomhan 위험하다, 위
험한
dark eodupda, eoduun 어둡
다, 어두운
date (of the month) naljja 날
짜
date of birth saengnyeonworil
생년월일

D

daughter ttal 딸
daughter-in-law myeoneuri 며느리
dawn saebyeok 새벽
day nat, nal 낮, 날
day after tomorrow more 모레
day before yesterday geujeokke 그저께
daydream, to gongsanghada 공상하다
day of the week yoil 요일
day off bibeon 비번
dead jukda, jugeun 죽다, 죽은
deaf gwiga meokda/meogeun 귀가 먹다/ 먹은
death jugeum 죽음
debt bit 빚
deceive, to sogida 속이다
December sibiwol 십이월
decide, to gyeoljjeonghada 결정하다
decision gyeoljjeong 결정
decline (get less), to soetoehada 쇠퇴하다
decline (refuse), to geojeolhada 거절하다
decorate, to kkumida 꾸미다
decrease, to julda 줄다
deep gipda, gipeun 깊다, 깊은
defeat, to chyeobusuda 처부수다
defecate, to baeseolhada 배설하다
defect gyeolham 결함
defend (in war), to bang.eohada 방어하다
defend (with words), to byeonhohada 변호하다
definite myeonghwakhada, myeonghwakan 명확하다/-한
degree, level deunggeup 등급
degrees (temperature) do 도

delay jiyeon 지연
delayed jiyeondoeda, jiyeondoen 지연되다, 지연된
delicious masitda, masinneun 맛있다, 맛있는
deliver, to baedalhada 배달하다
demand, to yoguhada 요구하다
democracy minjuju.ui 민주주의
dentist chikkwa(uisa) 치과(의사)
depart, to tteonada 떠나다
department bu, gwa 부, 과
department store baekhwajeom 백화점
departure chulbal 출발
depend on, to ...e dallyeo.itda ...에 달려있다
deposit (leave behind with someone), to matgida 맡기다
deposit (put money in the bank), to yegeumhada 예금하다
descendant jason 자손
describe, to myosahada 묘사하다
desert (arid land) samak 사막
desert, abandon, to beorida 버리다
desire yongmang 욕망
desire, to barada 바라다
desk chaeksang 책상
dessert dijeoteu 디저트
destination mokjeokji 목적지
destroy, to pagoehada 파괴하다
destroyed, ruined pagoedoeda, pagoedoen 파괴되다, 파괴된
detergent seje 세제
determined, stubborn hwakgohada, hwakgohan 확고하다/-한

develop (film), to
hyeonsanghada 현상하다
develop (happen), to
baljjeonhada, baljjeonsikida
발전하다, 발전시키다
development baljjeon, balttal
발전, 발달
diagonal daegakseon(ui) 대
각선(의)
diagonally daegakseoneuro
대각선으로
dial (telephone), to
jeonhwahada 전화하다
dialect saturi 사투리
diamond daiamondeu 다이
아몬드
diary, daybook ilgi 일기
diary, journal iljji 일지
dictionary sajeon 사전
die, to jukda 죽다
difference (discrepancy in figures) cha.aek 차액
difference (in quality) chai
차이
different, other dareuda,
dareun 다르다, 다른
difficult eoryeopda, eoryeo.un
어렵다, 어려운
dinner, evening meal
jeonyeok siksa 저녁 식사
dinner, to eat jeonyeok
siksahada 저녁 식사하다
dipper, ladle gukja 국자
direction banghyang 방향
director (of company) sajang
사장
dirt, filth omul 오물
dirty deoreopda, deoreo.un
더럽다, 더러운
disappointed silmanghada,
silmanghan 실망하다, 실
망한
disaster jaenan 재난
discount diseukaunteu 디스
카운트
discover, to balgyeonhada 발
견하다

discuss, to uinonhada 의논
하다
discussion uinon 의논
disease byeong 병
disgusting yeokgyeopda,
yeokgyeo.un 역겹다, 역겨운
dish (particular food) yori
요리
dish, platter jeopsi 접시
diskette diseuket 디스켓
dislike, to sireohada 싫어
하다
display jinyeol 진열
display, to jinyeolhada 진열
하다
distance geori 거리
disturb, to banghaehada 방
해하다
disturbance banghae 방해
divide, split up, to nanuda
나누다
divided by nanu.eojida,
nanu.eojin 나누어지다, 나누
어진
divorce, to ihonhada 이혼
하다
divorced ihonhada, ihonhan
이혼하다, 이혼한
do, perform an action, to
hada 하다
don't an 안
don't! geureoji maseyo! 그
러지 마세요!
don't mention it!
gwaenchanayo! 괜찮아요!
do one's best, to
choeseoneul dahada 최선을
다하다
doctor uisa 의사
document, letter munseo 문
서
dog gae 개
done (cooked) jal ikda/igeun
잘 익다/익은
done (finished) kkeunnada,
kkeunnan 끝나다, 끝난
door mun 문

double du bae 두 배
doubt, to uisimhada 의심하다
down, downward araero 아래로
downstairs araecheung 아래층
downtown sinae jungsimji 시내 중심지
dozen ...daseu ...다스
draw, to geurida 그리다
drawer seorap 서랍
drawing geurim 그림
dream kkum 꿈
dream, to kkumkkuda 꿈꾸다
dress, frock deureseu 드레스
dressed, to get ot ipda 옷 입다
dressing gown sillaebok 실내복
drink, refreshment eumnyo(su) 음료(수)
drink, to masida 마시다
drive (a car), to unjeonhada 운전하다
drop, to tteoreojida, tteoreotteurida 떨어지다, 떨어뜨리다
drought gamum 가뭄
drown, to iksahada 익사하다
drug (medicine) yak 약
drug (recreational) mayak 마약
drugstore, pharmacy yakguk 약국
drunk sul chwihada 술 취하다
dry mareuda, mareun 마르다, 마른
dry (weather) geonjohada, geonjohan 건조하다, 건조한
dry, to mallida 말리다
duck ori 오리
dull (boring) jiruhada, jiruhan 지루하다, 지루한

dull (weather) heurida, heurin 흐리다, 흐린
dumpling mandu 만두
during, for ...dong.an ...동안
dusk hwanghon 황혼
dust meonji 먼지
duty (import tax) gwanse 관세
duty (responsibility) chaegim 책임
DVD dibidi 디비디

E

each, every gakgak(ui) 각각(의)
ear gwi 귀
earrings gwigeori 귀걸이
earlier jeone 전에
early ireuda, ireun 이르다, 이른
early in the morning achim iljjik 아침 일찍
earn, to beolda 벌다
earth, soil heuk 흙
Earth, the world jigu 지구
earthquake jijin 지진
east dongjjok 동쪽
easy swipda, swiun 쉽다, 쉬운
eat, to meokda 먹다
economical gyeongjejeogida/-jeogin 경제적이다/-적인
economy gyeongje 경제
edge gajangjari 가장자리
educate, to gyoyukhada 교육하다
education gyoyuk 교육
effect, result gyeolgwa 결과
effort noryeok 노력
effort, to make an noryeokhada 노력하다
egg gyeran, al 계란, 알
eggplant, aubergine gaji 가지
eight yeodeol, pal 여덟, 팔
eighteen yeolyeodeol, sip.pal 열여덟, 십팔

eighty yeodeun, palsip 여든, 팔십
either ...(i)na ...eoneu han jjok ...(이)나 ... 어느 한 쪽
elbow palkkumchi 팔꿈치
elder sonwi(ui), yeonjangja 손위(의), 연장자
election seon.geo 선거
electric jeon.gi(ui) 전기(의)
electricity jeon.gi 전기
electronic jeonja(ui) 전자(의)
elegant uahada, uahan 우아 하다, 우아한
element yoso 요소
elephant kokkiri 코끼리
elevator ellibeiteo 엘리베이 터
eleven yeolhana, sibil 열하 나, 십일
elite elliteu 엘리트
else: anything else geubakke 그밖에
else: or else geureochi aneumyeon 그렇지 않으면
email (message) i meil 이 메일
email (system) i meil, jeonjaupyeon 이 메일, 전자 우편
email, to i meil bonaeda 이 메일 보내다
email address i meil juso 이 메일 주소
embarrassed danghwanghada /-haehada 당황하다/당황해 하다
embarrassing nancheohada /nancheohan 난처하다/난처한
embassy daesagwan 대사관
embrace, to kkyeo.anda 껴 안다
embroidered suno.eun 수놓 은
embroidery (ja)su (자)수
emergency bisang(satae) 비 상(사태)

emotion gamjeong 감정
employ, to goyonghada 고용 하다
employee pigoyong.in 피고 용인
employer goyongju 고용주
employment chwijik 취직
empty teong bida/bin 텅 비 다/빈
encourage, to gyeongnyeohada 격려하다
end kkeut 끝
end, to kkeunnada, kkeunnaeda 끝나다, 끝내다
enemy jeok 적
energy eneoji 에너지
engaged (telephone) tonghwajung.ida/-jung.in 통 화중이다/-중인
engaged (to be married) yakhonhada /-han 약혼하다/ -한
engine enjin 엔진
engineer gisa 기사
England yeongguk 영국
English yeong.eo 영어
engrave, to saegida 새기다
enjoy, to jeulgida 즐기다
enjoyable jeulgeopda, jeulgeo.un 즐겁다, 즐거운
enjoy oneself, to jeulgeopge bonaeda 즐겁게 보내다
enlarge, to hwakdaehada 확 대하다
enough chungbunhada, chungbunhan 충분하다, 충 분한
enquire, to mureoboda 물어 보다
enter, to deureogada 들어가 다
entire jeonche(ui) 전체(의)
entirety, whole jeonche 전 체
entrance, way in ipgu 입구
envelope bongtu 봉투

65

E

envious bureopda, bureowohada 부럽다, 부러워하다

environment, the hwan.gyeong 환경

envy bureo.um 부러움

equal gatda, gateun 같다, 같은

equality pyeongdeung 평등

error ereo, oryu 에러, 오류

escalator eseukeolleiteo 에스컬레이터

especially teukhi 특히

establish, set up, to seolliphada, se.uda 설립하다, 세우다

essay esei 에세이

estimate, to pyeongkkahada 평가하다

ethnic group minjok 민족

Europe yureop 유럽

even (also) ...jochado ...조차도

even (smooth) pyeongpyeonghada/-han 평평하다/-한

evening jeonyeok 저녁

event haengsa 행사

ever, to have done -(eu)n jeogi itda -(으)ㄴ 적이 있다

every modeun, mae... 모든, 매...

everybody, everyone modeun saram 모든 사람

every kind of modeun jongnyu.ui 모든 종류의

everything modeun geot 모든 것

every time maebeon, -(eu)l ttaemada 매번, -(으)ㄹ 때마다

everywhere eodideunji, modeun got 어디든지, 모든 곳

exact, exactly? jeonghwakhada/-han/-hi 정확하다/-한/-히

exactly! just so! baro geugeoyeyo! 바로 그거예요!

exam, test siheom 시험

examine, to geomtohada, jinchalhada 검토하다, 진찰하다

example ye 예

example, for yereul deuljamyeon 예를 들자면

excellent usuhada, usuhan 우수하다, 우수한

except ...eul/reul je.oehago ...을/를 제외하고

exchange (money, opinions), to gyohwanhada 교환하다

exchange rate hwannyul 환율

excited sini nada, sini nan 신이 나다, 신이 난

exciting sinnada, sinnaneun 신나다, 신나는

excuse me! sillyehamnida! 실례합니다!

excuse me! (apology) mianhamnida! 미안합니다!

exist, to jonjaehada 존재하다

exit, way out chulgu 출구

expand, grow larger, to hwakjanghada 확장하다

expect, to gidaehada 기대하다

expense biyong 비용

expenses jichulgeum 지출금

expensive bissada, bissan 비싸다, 비싼

experience gyeongheom 경험

experience, to gyeongheomhada 경험하다

expert jeonmun.ga 전문가

explain, to seolmyeonghada 설명하다

export suchul(pum) 수출(품)

export, to suchulhada 수출하다

express, state, to pyohyeonhada 표현하다

extension (telephone)
naeseon 내선
extra chuga(ui) 추가(의)
extremely geukdoro 극도로
eye nun 눈
eyebrow nunsseop 눈썹
eyeglasses, spectacles
an.gyeong 안경

F

fabric, textile jingmul 직물
face eolgul 얼굴
face, to jingmyeonhada 직면
하다
fact sasil 사실
factory gongjang 공장
fail, to silpaehada, nakjehada
실패하다, 낙제하다
failure silpae, nakje 실패, 낙
제
fall (season) ga.eul 가을
fall, to tteoreojida 떨어지다
fall over, to neomeojida 넘어
지다
false (imitation) gajjaida, gajja
가짜이다, 가짜
false (not true) geojisida,
geojit 거짓이다, 거짓
family gajok 가족
famine gigeun 기근
famous yumyeonghada,
yumyeonghan 유명하다, 유
명한
fan (admirer) paen 팬
fan (for cooling) buchae 부
채
fancy jangsigi manta/maneun
장식이 많다/많은
far meolda, meon 멀다, 먼
fare yogeum 요금
fast, rapid ppareuda, ppareun
빠르다, 빠른
fast, to dansikhada 단식하다
fat, grease jibang 지방
fat, plump ttungttunghada/-
han 뚱뚱하다/-한
father abeoji 아버지

father-in-law siabeoji, jang.in
시아버지, 장인
fault jalmot 잘못
fax (machine) paekseu(gi) 팩
스스(기)
fax (message) paekseu 팩스
fax, to paekseu bonaeda 팩
스 보내다
fear museo.um 무서움
February iwol 이월
fee susuryo, biyong 수수료,
비용
feed, to meogida 먹이다
feel, to neukkida 느끼다
feeling neukkim 느낌
female yeoseong 여성
fence dam, ultari 담, 울타리
ferry bae 배
fertile biokhada, biokan 비옥
하다, 비옥한
festival janchi, chukje 잔치,
축제
fetch, to gajyeo.oda 가져오
다
fever yeol 열
few geo.i eopda/eomneun
거의 없다/없는
fiancé yakhonja 약혼자
fiancée yakhonnyeo 약혼녀
field, empty space gongteo,
gyeonggijang 공터, 경기장
fierce sanapda, sanaun 사납
다, 사나운
fifteen yeoldaseot, sibo 열다
섯, 십오
fifty swin, osip 쉰, 오십
fight (physically), to ssauda
싸우다
fight over, to ...e daehae
nonjaenghada ...에 대해 논
쟁하다
figure, number sujja 숫자
fill, to chae.uda 채우다
fill out (form), to
jakseonghada 작성하다
film (camera) pilleum 필름
film, movie yeonghwa 영화

F

final majimak(ui) 마지막(의)
finally machimnae 마침내
find, to chatda 찾다
fine (okay) jota, jo.eun 좋다, 좋은
fine (punishment) beolgeum 벌금
finger sonkkarak 손가락
finish kkeut 끝
finish off, to kkeunnaeda 끝내다
finished kkeunnada, kkeunnan 끝나다, 끝난
finished (none left) tteoreojida 떨어지다
fire bul 불
fire someone, to haegohada 해고하다
fireworks bulkkonnori 불꽃놀이
firm (definite) hwakgohada, hwakgohan 확고하다, 확고한
firm (mattress) dandanhada, dandanhan 단단하다, 단단한
firm, company hoesa 회사
first cheot beonjjae 첫 번째
first, earlier, beforehand meonjeo 먼저
fish mulkkogi, saengseon 물고기, 생선
fish, to gogi japda 고기 잡다
fish paste eomuk 어묵
fish sauce aekjeot 액젓
fit, to kkok matda 꼭 맞다
fitting, suitable eo.ullida, eo.ullineun 어울리다, 어울리는
five daseot, o 다섯, 오
fix (a time, appointment), to jeonghada 정하다
fix (repair), to gochida 고치다
flag gippal 깃발
flashlight, torch sonjeondeung 손전등

flat, apartment apateu 아파트
flat, smooth pyeongpyeonghada /-han 평평하다/ 평평한
flight bihaeng 비행
flood hongsu 홍수
floor maru, cheung 마루, 층
flour milkkaru 밀가루
flower kkot 꽃
flu dokgam 독감
fluent yuchanghada, yuchanghan 유창하다, 유창한
flute peulluteu 플루트
fly (insect) pari 파리
fly, to nalda 날다
fog an.gae 안개
fold, to jeopda 접다
follow along, to jjuk ttaragada 쭉 따라가다
follow behind, to dwittaragada 뒤따라가다
following da.eum 다음
fond of, to be joahada 좋아하다
food eumsik 음식
foot bal 발
for ...eul/reul wihan, ...dong.an ... 을/를 위한, ...동안
forbid, to geumhada 금하다
forbidden geumjidoeda, geumjidoen 금지되다, 금지된
force him 힘
force, compel, to gang.yohada 강요하다
forehead ima 이마
foreign oeguk(ui) 외국(의)
foreigner oegugin 외국인
forest sup 숲
for ever yeong.wonhi 영원히
forget, to itda 잊다
forgive, to yongseohada 용서하다
forgiveness, mercy youngseo 용서

forgotten ichyeojida, ichyeojin 잊혀지다, 잊혀진
fork pokeu 포크
form (application) sincheongseo 신청서
form (shape) moyang 모양
form (to fill out), to jakseonghada 작성하다
fortress yosae 요새
fortunately dahaenghi 다행히
forty maheun, sasip 마흔, 사십
forward apeuro 앞으로
four net, sa 넷, 사
fourteen yeolnet, sipsa 열넷, 십사
free, independent dongniphada, dongnipan 독립하다, 독립한
freedom jayu 자유
free of charge muryo(ui) 무료(의)
free of restraints jayuropda, jayuroun 자유롭다, 자유로운
freeze, to eol(li)da 얼(리)다
frequent binbeonhada, binbeonhan 빈번하다, 빈번한
fresh sinseonhada, sinseonhan 신선하다, 신선한
Friday geumyoil 금요일
fried twigin 튀긴
friend chin.gu 친구
friendly, outgoing sagyojeogida, sagyojeogin 사교적이다/-적인
frightened geommeokda, geommeogeun 겁먹다, 겁먹은
from ...eseo, ...buteo ...에서, ...부터
front jeongmyeon 정면
front: in front of ...ape(seo) ... 앞에(서)
frown, to jjinggeurida 찡그리다

frozen eolda, eon 얼다, 언
fruit gwail 과일
fry, to twigida 튀기다
fulfill, to suhaenghada 수행하다
full gadeuk chada/chan 가득 차다/찬
full, eaten one's fill baebureuda 배부르다
fun, to have jaemiitge bonaeda 재미있게 보내다
function, to work jagyonghada 작용하다
funds, funding gigeum 기금
funeral jangnyesik 장례식
fungus gompang.i 곰팡이
funny jaemiitda, jaemiinneun 재미있다, 재미있는
furniture gagu 가구
further, additional geu isang.ui 그 이상의
fussy kkadaropda, kkadaroun 까다롭다, 까다로운
future, in future mirae 미래

G

gamble dobak 도박
game geim 게임
garage (for parking) chago 차고
garage (for repairs) jeongbiso 정비소
garbage sseuregi 쓰레기
garden, park gong.won 공원
garden, yard jeong.won 정원
garlic maneul 마늘
garment ot 옷
gasoline gasollin, gireum 가솔린, 기름
gasoline station juyuso 주유소
gate mun 문
gather, to mo.euda, moida 모으다, 모이다

G

gender seongbyeol 성별
general, all-purpose
  ilbanjeogida, ilbanjeogin 일반
  적이다/-적인
generally ilbanjeogeuro 일반
  적으로
generous neogeureopda,
  neogeureoun 너그럽다, 너그
  러운
gentle jeomjanta, jeomjaneun
  점잖다, 점잖은
genuine jinjja(ui) 진짜(의)
geography jiri(hak) 지리(학)
germ se.gyun 세균
gesture jeseucheo 제스처
get, receive, to eotda 얻다
get off (transport), to naerida
  내리다
get on (transport), to tada
  타다
get up (from bed), to
  ireonada 일어나다
get well soon! got
  hoebokhaseyo! 곧 회복하세
  요!
ghost gwisin, yuryeong 귀신,
  유령
giant geo.in, geodaehan 거
  인, 거대한
gift seonmul 선물
ginger saenggang 생강
girl so.nyeo 소녀
girlfriend yeojachin.gu 여자
  친구
give, to juda 주다
given name ireum 이름
glad gippeuda, gippeun 기쁘
  다, 기쁜
glass (for drinking) keop 컵
glass (material) yuri 유리
glasses, spectacles
  an.gyeong 안경
gloves janggap 장갑
glutinous rice chapssal 찹쌀
go, to gada 가다
go along, join in, to
  chamyeohada 참여하다

go around, visit, to gaboda
  가보다
go back , to doragada 돌아
  가다
go for a walk, to
  sanchaekhada 산책하다
go home, to jibe gada 집에
  가다
go out (fire, candle), to
  kkeojida 꺼지다
go out, exit, to nagada 나가
  다
go to bed, to jada/jareogada
  자다/자러가다
go up, climb, to ollagada 올
  라가다
goal mokpyo 목표
goat yeomso 염소
God haneunim 하느님
god sin 신
goddess yeosin 여신
gold geum 금
golf golpeu 골프
gone, finished kkeunnada 끝
  나다
good jota, jo.eun 좋다, 좋은
goods sangpum 상품
goodbye (to a person
  leaving) annyeonghi gaseyo
  안녕히 가세요
goodbye (to a person
  staying) annyeonghi
  gyeseyo 안녕히 계세요
good luck! haeng.uneul
  bimnida! 행운을 빕니다!
goodness! eomeona,
  sesang.e! 어머나, 세상에!
goose geowi 거위
government jeongbu 정부
gradually jeomchajeogeuro
  점차적으로
grain gongmul 곡물
grammar munppeop 문법
grand, great aju keuda/keun
  아주 크다/큰
grandchild sonja, sonnyeo
  손자, 손녀

granddaughter sonnyeo 손녀

grandfather harabeoji, jobu 할아버지, 조부

grandmother halmeoni, jomo 할머니, 조모

grandparents jobumo 조부모

grandson sonja 손자

grapes podo 포도

grass pul 풀

grateful gomapda, gomaun 고맙다, 고마운

grave mudeom 무덤

great, impressive daedanhada, daedanhan 대단하다, 대단한

green pureuda, pureun 푸르다, 푸른

green beans wandukong 완두콩

greens yachae 야채

greet, to insahada 인사하다

greetings insamal 인사말

grey hoesaek(ui) 회색(의)

grill, to gupda 굽다

ground, earth ttang 땅

group geurup 그룹

grow, be growing (plant), to jarada 자라다

grow, cultivate, to jaebaehada 재배하다

grow larger, to keojida 커지다

grow up (child), to seongjanghada 성장하다

guarantee bojeung 보증

guarantee, to bojeunghada 보증하다

guard, to jikida 지키다

guess, to chucheukhada 추측하다

guest sonnim 손님

guesthouse yeogwan 여관

guest of honor gwibin 귀빈

guide, lead gaideu 가이드

guidebook annaeseo 안내서

guilty (of a crime) yujoe.ida, yujoe.in 유죄이다, 유죄인

guilty, to feel joechaekgameul neukkida 죄책감을 느끼다

gun chong 총

H

habit beoreut 버릇

hair meori(karak) 머리(카락)

half ban 반

hall hol 홀

hammer mangchi 망치

hand son 손

handicap jang.ae 장애

handicraft sugong.ye 수공예

handkerchief sonsugeon 손수건

handle sonjabi 손잡이

hand out, to nanu.eojuda 나누어주다

hand over, to neomgyeojuda 넘겨주다

handsome jalsaenggida, jalsaenggin 잘생기다, 잘생긴

handy pyeollihada, pyeollihan 편리하다, 편리한

hang, to geolda 걸다

happen, occur, to ireonada 일어나다

happened, what happened? museun irieyo? 무슨 일이에요?

happening, incident sakkeon 사건

happy haengbokhada, hangbokan 행복하다, 행복한

happy birthday! saeng.il chukhahamnida! 생일 축하합니다!

happy new year! saehae bok mani badeuseyo! 새해 복 많이 받으세요!

harbor hanggu 항구

hard (difficult) eoryeopda, eoryeo.un 어렵다, 어려운

hard (solid) dandanhada, dandanhan 단단하다, 단단한

H

ENGLISH—KOREAN

hard disk hadeudiseukeu 하드디스크

hardly geo.i -ji anta 거의 -지 않다

hardware cheolmul 철물

hardworking, industrious geunmyeonhada/-han 근면하다/-한

harm hae 해

harmful haeropda, haero.un 해롭다, 해로운

harmonious johwadoeda, johwadoen 조화되다, 조화된

hat moja 모자

hate, to miwohada 미워하다

hatred jeung.o 증오

have, own, to itda 있다

have been somewhere, to ga bonjeogi itda 가 본적이 있다

have done something, to da haetda 다 했다

have to, must -a/eoya hada -아/어야 하다

he, him geu 그

head meori 머리

head for, toward, to ...(eu)ro hyanghada ...(으)로 향하다

headquarters bonbu 본부

healthy geon.ganghada, geon.ganghan 건강하다, 건강한

hear, to deutda 듣다

heart simjang, ma.eum 심장, 마음

heat, to de.uda 데우다

heaven cheon.guk 천국

heavy mugeopda, mugeo.un 무겁다, 무거운

height nopi 높이

hello! (on phone) yeoboseyo! 여보세요!

hello, hi annyeonghaseyo 안녕하세요

help! dowajuseyo! 도와주세요!

help, to dopda 돕다

her, hers geunyeo.ui, geunyeo.ui geot 그녀의, 그녀의 것

here yeogi, iri(ro) 여기, 이리(로)

hesitate, to jujeohada 주저하다

hidden sumgyeojida, sumgyeojin 숨겨지다, 숨겨진

hide, to sum(gi)da 숨(기)다

high nopda, nopeun 높다, 높은

highway gosokdoro 고속도로

hill eondeok 언덕

hinder, to banghaehada 방해하다

hindrance banghae 방해

hire, to goyonghada 고용하다

his geu.ui, geu.ui geot 그의, 그의 것

history yeoksa 역사

hit, strike, to chida, ttaerida 치다, 때리다

hobby chwimi 취미

hold, grasp, to butjapda 붙잡다

hold back, to eokjehada 억제하다

hole gumeong 구멍

holiday (a day off) hyu.il 휴일

holiday (festival) myeongjeol 명절

holiday (vacation) hyuga 휴가

holidays, vacation (school) banghak 방학

holy sinseonghada, sinseonghan 신성하다, 신성한

home, house jip 집

homesickness hyangsuppyeong 향수병

honest jeongjikhada, jeongjikan 정직하다, 정직한

honey kkul 꿀
Hong Kong hongkong 홍콩
honor myeong.ye 명예
hope, to barada 바라다
hopefully barageonde 바라 건대
horizon supyeongseon, jipyeongseon 수평선, 지평선
horse mal 말
hospital byeong.won 병원
host ju.in 주인
hot (spicy) maepda, mae.un 맵다, 매운
hot (temperature) deopda, deo.un 덥다, 더운
hotel hotel 호텔
hot spring oncheon 온천
hour sigan 시간
house jip 집
housewife jubu 주부
how? eotteokeyo? 어떻게요?
how are you? annyeonghaseyo? 안녕하세요?
however geureona 그러나
how long? eolmana oraeyo? 얼마나 오래요?
how many? eolmana maniyo? 얼마나 많이요?
how much? eolmayeyo? 얼마예요?
how old? myeot sarieyo? 몇 살이에요?
huge geodaehada, geodaehan 거대하다, 거대한
human in.gan 인간
humid mudeopda, mudeo.un 무덥다, 무더운
humorous utgida, utgineun 웃기다, 웃기는
hundred baek 백
hundred thousand simman 십만
hungry baegopeuda, baegopeun 배고프다, 배고픈
hurry up! ppalliyo! 빨리요!

hurt (cause pain), to apeuge hada 아프게 하다
hurt (injured) dachida, dachin 다치다, 다친
husband nampyeon 남편
hut, shack odumak 오두막

I, me na, nae, jeo, je 나, 내, 저, 제
ice eoreum 얼음
ice cream aiseu keurim 아이스 크림
idea saenggak 생각
identical gatda, gateun 같다, 같은
if manil -(eu)myeon 만일 -(으)면
ignore, to musihada 무시하다
ignorant musikhada, musikan 무식하다, 무식한
ill, sick apeuda, apeun 아프다, 아픈
illegal bulppeobida, bulppeop 불법이다, 불법
illness byeong 병
imagine, to sangsanghada 상상하다
immediately got 곧
impolite muryehada, muryehan 무례하다, 무례한
import su.ip 수입
import, to su.iphada 수입하다
importance jung.yoseong 중요성
important jung.yohada, jung.yohan 중요하다, 중요한
impossible bulganeunghada/-han 불가능하다/-한
impression, to make an insang.eul juda 인상을 주다
impressive insangjeogida, insangjeogin 인상적이다, 인상적인
in, at (place) ...e(seo) ...에 (서)

in (time, years) ...e ... 에
in addition gedaga 게다가
incense hyang 향
incident sakkeon 사건
included, including
pohamdoen, pohamhaeseo
포함된, 포함해서
income su.ip 수입
increase jeungga 증가
increase, to jeunggahada 증
가하다
indeed! geureomyo! 그럼요!
independent dongnip(ui) 독
립(의)
indigenous tochak(ui) 토착
(의)
indigestion sohwabullyang
소화불량
individual gaein(ui) 개인(의)
Indonesia indonesia 인도네
시아
industry saneop 산업
inexpensive ssada, ssan 싸
다, 싼
infect gamyeomsikida 감염시
키다
inflation inpeulleisyeon 인플
레이션
influence yeonghyang 영향
influence, to yeonghyang.eul
juda 영향을 주다
inform, to allida 알리다
information jeongbo 정보
information booth annaeso
안내소
inhabitant jumin 주민
inject, to jusahada 주사하다
injection jusa 주사
injured dachida, dachin 다치
다, 다친
injury busang 부상
ink ingkeu 잉크
innocent gyeolbaekhada,
gyeolbaekan 결백하다, 결백
한
in order that, so that -gi
wihaeseo -기 위해서

insane michida, michin 미치
다, 미친
insect beolle 벌레
insert, to sabiphada 삽입하
다
inside anjjok 안쪽
inside of ...ane(seo) ... 안에
(서)
insist, to jujanghada 주장하
다
inspect, to josahada 조사하
다
install, to seolchihada 설치
하다
instead of ...daesine ... 대신
에
instinct bonneung 본능
instruct, tell to do
something, to jisihada 지시
하다
insult moyok 모욕
insult someone, to
moyokhada 모욕하다
insurance boheom 보험
intend, to -(eu)ryeogo hada -
(으)려고 하다
intended for ...wihae
goandoeda ... 위해 고안되다
intention uido 의도
interest (money) ija 이자
interested in gwansimi itda/
inneun 관심이 있다/있는
interesting jaemiitda,
jaemiinneun 재미있다, 재미
있는
international gukjejeogida,
gukje(jeogin) 국제적이다/-
(적인)
Internet inteonet 인터넷
interpreter tong.yeoksa 통역
사
intersection gyocha(ro) 교차
(로)
interview myeonjeop 면접
into ...aneuro ... 안으로
introduce someone, to
sogaehada 소개하다

K

invent, to balmyeonghada 발명하다
invitation chodae 초대
invite (ask along), to oragohada 오라고하다
invite (formally), to chodaehada 초대하다
invoice cheongguseo 청구서
involve, to pohamhada 포함하다
involved gwallyeondoeda/-doen 관련되다/-된
Ireland aillaendeu 아일랜드
iron cheol 철
iron (clothing), to darida 다리다
is (equation) ida 이다
is (exist) itda 있다
Islam iseullamgyo 이슬람교
island seom 섬
item, individual thing ...gae ...개
ivory sang.a 상아

J

jacket jaket 자켓
jail gamok 감옥
jam jaem 잼
January irwol 일월
Japan ilbon 일본
Japanese ilbon saram, ilboneo 일본 사람, 일본어
jaw teok 턱
jealous jiltuhada, jiltuhaneun 질투하다, 질투하는
jealousy jiltu 질투
jewellery boseok 보석
job jigeop, il 직업, 일
join together, to yeon.gyeolhada 연결하다
join, go along, to gaiphada 가입하다
joke nongdam 농담
journalist eollonin 언론인
journey yeohaeng 여행
joy gippeum 기쁨

jug, pitcher jujeonja 주전자
juice jyuseu 쥬스
July chirwol 칠월
jump, to jeompeuhada 점프하다
June yuwol 유월
jungle jeonggeul 정글
jury baesimwon 배심원
just, fair gongjeonghada/-han 공정하다/-한
just, only danji, ...man 단지, ...만
justice jeong.i 정의
just now baro jigeum 바로 지금

K

keep, to jikida, bogwanhada 지키다, 보관하다
key (computer) ki 키
key (to room) yeolsoe 열쇠
keyboard (of computer) kibodeu 키보드
kidney sinjang 신장
kidney beans gangnangkong 강낭콩
kill, murder, to jugida 죽이다
kilogram killogeuraem 킬로그램
kilometer killomiteu 킬로미터
kind (of persons) chinjeolhada, chinjeolhan 친절하다/-한
kind, type jongnyu 종류
king wang 왕
kiss kiseu 키스
kiss, to kiseuhada 키스하다
kitchen bu.eok 부엌
kiwi fruit kiwi 키위
knee mureup 무릎
knife kal 칼
knock, to dudeurida 두드리다
know, to alda 알다
know, be acquainted with, to ...e iksukhada ...에 익숙하다

knowledge jisik 지식
Korea hanguk 한국,
  daehanminguk 대한민국
Korea, North bukhan 북한
Korea, South namhan 남한
Korean han.guk saram,
  han.gugeo 한국 사람, 한
  국어

L

labor nodong 노동
lacking -i/ga eopda/eomneun
  -이/가 없다/없는
ladder sadari 사다리
lady sungnyeo 숙녀
lake hosu 호수
lamb, mutton yanggogi 양고
  기
lamp deung 등
land ttang 땅
land (plane), to
  changnyukhada 착륙하다
lane (alley) golmokgil 골목길
lane (of a highway) chaseon
  차선
language mal, eoneo 말, 언어
large keuda, keun 크다, 큰
last, to jisokhada 지속하다
last night jinan bam 지난 밤
last week jinan ju 지난 주
last year jangnyeon 작년
late neutda, neujeun 늦다,
  늦은
late at night bamneukke 밤
  늦게
lately choegeun(e) 최근(에)
later najung.e 나중에
laugh, to utda 웃다
laugh at, to biutda 비웃다
laundry setakso 세탁소
laws, legislation beop 법
lawyer byeonhosa 변호사
layer cheung 층
lay the table, to siksa
  junbihada 식사 준비하다
lazy ge.eureuda, ge.eureun
  게으르다, 게으른

lead (to be a leader), to
  jidohada 지도하다
**lead (to guide someone
  somewhere), to** annaehada
  안내하다
leader jidoja 지도자
leaf ip 잎
leak, to saeda 새다
learn, to bae.uda 배우다
least (smallest amount)
  choeso 최소
least: at least jeogeodo 적어
  도
leather gajuk 가죽
leave, depart, to tteonada
  떠나다
leave behind by accident, to
  dugo oda(come)/gada(go)
  두고 오다/가다
**leave behind for safekeeping,
  to** matgida 맡기다
leave behind on purpose, to
  namgida 남기다
lecture gang.ui 강의
lecturer (at university)
  gangsa (gyosu) 강사 (교수)
left, remaining namda,
  nameun 남다, 남은
left-hand side oenjjok 왼쪽
leg dari 다리
legal hapbeopjeogida/-jeogin
  합법적이다/-적인
legend jeonseol 전설
lemon remon 레몬
lend, to billyeojuda 빌려주다
length giri 길이
less (smaller amount) deo
  jeokda/jeogeun 더 적다/적은
less, minus ...eopda,
  ...eomneun, ... 없다, ... 없는
lessen, reduce, to jurida 줄
  이다
lesson gwa, su.eop 과, 수업
let, allow, to -ge hada -게 하
  다
let's (suggestion) -(eu)p sida
  -(으)ㅂ시다

let someone know, to allida
알리다
letter pyeonji 편지
level (even, flat)
pyeongpyeonghada/-han 평
평하다/-한
level (height) nopi 높이
level (standard) sujun 수준
liberty jayu 자유
library doseogwan 도서관
licence (for driving)
myeonheojjeung 면허증
licence, permit heoga 허가
lick, to haltta 핥다
lid ttukkeong 뚜껑
lie, tell a falsehood, to
geojinmalhada 거짓말하다
lie down, to nupda 눕다
life saengmyeong 생명
lifetime pyeongsaeng,
insaeng 평생, 인생
lift, elevator seungganggi 승
강기
lift (ride in car) cha taewojum
차 태워줌
lift, raise, to (deureo)ollida
(들어)올리다
light (bright) bakda, balgeun
밝다, 밝은
light (lamp) bul 불
light (not heavy) gabyeopda,
gabyeo.un 가볍다, 가벼운
lighter raiteo 라이터
lightning beon.gae 번개
like, as ...cheoreom ...처럼
like, be pleased by, to
joahada 좋아하다
likewise machan.gajiro 마찬
가지로
limit jehan 제한
limit, to jehanhada
제한하다
line (mark) seon 선
line (queue) jul 줄
line up, to julseoda 줄서다
lips ipsul 입술
liquor, alcohol sul 술

list myeongdan 명단
listen, to deutda 듣다
literature munhak 문학
little (not much) jeokda,
jeogeun 적다, 적은
little (small) jakda, jageun
작다, 작은
live (be alive) sarainneun
살아있는
live (stay in a place), to salda
살다
liver gan 간
load jim 짐
load up, to sitda 싣다
loan daebu 대부
located, to be wichihada 위
치하다
lock jamulsoe 자물쇠
lock, to jamgeuda 잠그다
locked jamgida, jamgin 잠기
다, 잠긴
lodge, small hotel yeogwan
여관
lonely oeropda, oeroun 외롭
다, 외로운
long (length) gilda, gin 길다,
긴
long (time) orae, oraen 오래,
오랜
look! boseyo! 보세요!
look at, see, to boda 보다
look, seem, appear, to -
ge/...(eu)ro boida -게/...(으)
로 보이다
look after, to dolboda 돌보다
look for, to chatda 찾다
look like, to ...cheoreom
boida ...처럼 보이다
look out! josimhaseyo! 조심
하세요!
look up (find in book), to
chajaboda 찾아보다
loose (not in packet) nat
gae(ui) 낱 개(의)
loose (wobbly)
heundeulheundeulhada/-han
흔들흔들하다/-한

L

lose, be defeated, to jida 지다
lose, mislay, to ireobeorida
잃어버리다
lose money, to sonhaeboda
손해보다
lost (can't find way) gireul
ilta/ireun 길을 잃다/잃은
lost (missing) ireobeorin 잃
어버린
lost property bunsilmul 분실
물
lots of maneun 많은
lottery bokgwon 복권
loud soriga keuda/keun 소리
가 크다/큰
love sarang 사랑
love, to saranghada 사랑하다
lovely sarangseureopda,
sarangseureo.un 사랑스럽다
/-스러운
low natda, najeun 낮다, 낮은
luck un 운
lucky un jota/jo.eun 운 좋다
/좋은
luggage yeohaenggabang 여
행가방
lunch, midday meal jeomsim
siksa 점심 식사
lunch, to eat jeomsim
siksahada 점심 식사하다
lungs pye 폐
luxurious sachiseureopda,
sachiseureo.un 사치스럽다/-
스러운

M

machine gigye 기계
machinery gigyeryu 기계류
mad michida, michin 미치다,
미친
madam (term of address)
bu.in 부인
magazine japji 잡지
mah jong majak 마작
mail, post upyeonmul 우편
물
mail, to buchida 부치다

main, most important
juyohan 주요한
mainly juro 주로
major (important)
jung.yohada, jung.yohan 중
요하다, 중요한
make, to mandeulda 만들다
make, do, to ...hada ...하다
make up, invent, to
mandeulda 만들다
Malaysia malleisia 말레이
시아
male namseong 남성
man namja 남자
manage, succeed, to
cheorihaenaeda 처리해내다
manager bujang 부장,
gwallichaegimja 관리책임자
mango manggo 망고
manner bangbeop 방법
manners yejeol, yei 예절,
예의
manufacture, to jejohada 제
조하다
many, much manta, maneun
많다, 많은
map jido 지도
March samwol 삼월
market sijang 시장
married gyeolhonhada,
gyeolhonhan 결혼하다, 결
혼한
marry, get married, to
gyeolhonhada 결혼하다
mask tal, gamyeon 탈, 가면
massage, to masajihada 마
사지하다
mat kkalgae 깔개
match, game sihap 시합
matches seongnyang 성냥
material, ingredient jaeryo
재료
matter, issue munje 문제
matter, it doesn't
sanggwaneopda 상관없다
mattress maeteuriseu 매트
리스

May owol 오월
may -a/eodo jota -아/어도 좋다
maybe ama 아마
meal siksa 식사, bap 밥
mean (cruel) biyeolhada, biyeolhan 비열하다, 비열한
mean (intend), to -(eu)ryeogo hada -(으)려고 하다
mean (word), to uimihada 의미하다
meaning uimi, tteut 의미, 뜻
meanwhile geu dong.an(e) 그 동안(에)
measure, to jaeda 재다
measurement chisu 치수
measure out, to jae.eonaeda 재어내다
meat gogi 고기
meatball gogi wanja 고기 완자
medical uihak(ui) 의학(의)
medicine yak 약
meet, to mannada 만나다
meeting moim 모임
melon chamoe 참외
member hoewon 회원
memories gi.eok, chu.eok 기억, 추억
mend, to gochida 고치다
menstruate, to saengnihada 생리하다
mention, to malhada 말하다
menu menyu 메뉴
merely danji 단지
mess, in a eongmang.ida eongmang.in 엉망이다, 엉망인
message mesiji 메시지
metal geumsok 금속
method bangbeop 방법
midday jeong.o 정오
middle, center junggan, gaunde 중간, 가운데
middle: be in the middle of doing -neun jung.e -는 중(에)

midnight hanbamjjung 한밤중
mild (not severe) gabyeo.un, yakganui 가벼운, 약간의
mild (not spicy) sunhada, sunhan 순하다, 순한
military gunsa(ui) 군사(의)
milk uyu 우유
million baengman 백만
mind, brain saenggak 생각
mind, be displeased, to sin.gyeong sseuda 신경 쓰다
minibus minibeoseu 미니버스
minor (not important) sasohada, sasohan 사소하다, 사소한
minus maineoseu 마이너스
minute bun 분
mirror geo.ul 거울
misfortune bulhaeng 불행
miss (bus, flight), to nochida 놓치다
miss (loved one), to geuriwohada 그리워하다
missing (absent) eopseojida, eopseojin 없어지다, 없어진
missing (person) haengbangbulmyeongdoeda/ -doen 행방불명되다/-된
mist angae 안개
mistake silssu 실수
mistaken teullida, teullin 틀리다, 틀린
misunderstanding ohae 오해
mix, to seokda 섞다
mixed seokkida, seokkin 섞이다, 섞인
mobile phone haendeupon 핸드폰
modern hyeondae(ui) 현대(의)
modest, simple susuhada, susuhan 수수하다, 수수한
moment (instant) sun.gan 순간

M

moment (just a moment)!
jamkkanmanyo! 잠깐만요!
Monday woryoil 월요일
money don 돈
monitor (of computer)
moniteo 모니터
monkey wonsung.i 원숭이
month dal 달
monument ginyeommul 기
념물
mood gibun 기분
moon dal 달
more (comparative) deo 더
more of (things) deo
maneun 더 많은
more or less daso 다소
morning achim 아침
mosquito mogi 모기
most (superlative) gajang,
jeil 가장, 제일
most (the most of) daebubun
대부분
mostly juro 주로
moth nabang 나방
mother eomeoni 어머니
mother-in-law sieomeoni,
jangmo 시어머니, 장모
motor, engine moteo 모터
motorcycle otobai 오토바이
motor vehicle jadongcha 자
동차
mountain san 산
mouse (animal) saengjwi 생
쥐
mouse (computer) mauseu
마우스
moustache kossuyeom 콧수
염
mouth ip 입
move, to isahada 이사하다
**move from one place to
another, to** omgida 옮기다
movement, motion dongjak
동작
movie yeonghwa 영화
movie house yeonghwagwan
영화관

much, many manta, maneun
많다, 많은
muscle geunyuk 근육
museum bangmulgwan 박물
관
mushroom beoseot 버섯
music eumak 음악
Muslim iseullamgyodo 이슬
람교도
must -a/eoya hada -아/어야
하다
my, mine nae, nae geot 내,
내 것
myth sinhwa 신화

N

nail (finger, toe) sontop,
baltop 손톱, 발톱
nail (spike) mot 못
naked beolgeobeotda/-
beoseun 벌거벗다/-벗은
name ireum 이름
narrow jopda, jobeun 좁다,
좁은
nation, country gukga 국가
national gukga(ui) 국가(의)
nationality gukjeok 국적
natural jayeon(ui) 자연(의)
nature jayeon 자연
naughty beoreuteopda,
beoreuteomneun 버릇없다/-
없는
nearby gakkaie 가까이에
nearly geo.ui 거의
neat, orderly danjeonghada,
danjeonghan 단정하다, 단
정한
necessary piryohada, piryohan
필요하다, 필요한
neck mok 목
necklace mokgeori 목걸이
necktie nektai 넥타이
need piryo 필요
need, to piryohada 필요하다
needle baneul 바늘
neighbor iut(saram) 이웃(사
람)

neither eoneu jjokdo ...anida/-ji anta 어느 쪽도 ...아니다/-지 않다

neither...nor ...do ...do anida/-ji anta /...도 /...도 ...아니다/-지 않다

nephew joka 조카

nervous chojohaehada, chojohaehaneun 초조해하다 /-하는

nest dungji 둥지

net geumul, neteu 그물, 네트

network ...mang, neteuwokeu ...망, 네트워크

never gyeolko ...anida/-ji anta 결코 ...아니다/-지 않다

never mind! sin.gyeong sseuji maseyo! 신경 쓰지 마세요!

nevertheless geuraedo 그래도

new saeropda, sae(roun) 새 롭다, 새(로운)

news nyuseu 뉴스

newspaper sinmun 신문

New Zealand nyujillaendeu 뉴질랜드

next (in line, sequence) da.eum(ui) 다음(의)

next to ...yeope ... 옆에

next week da.eumju 다음주

next year naenyeon 내년

nice meotjida, meotjin 멋지 다, 멋진

niece jokattal 조카딸

night bam 밤

nightclothes jamot 잠옷

nightly yagan 야간

nine ahop, gu 아홉, 구

nineteen yeorahop, sipgu 열 아홉, 십구

ninety aheun, gusip 아흔, 구십

no (answer) anio 아니오

no, not (with nouns) ...anida ... 아니다

no, not (with verbs and adjectives) an, -ji anta 안, -지 않다

nobody amudo -ji anta 아무 도 -지 않다

noise so.eum 소음

noisy sikkeureopda, sikkeureoun 시끄럽다, 시끄 러운

nonsense neonsenseu 넌센 스

noodles guksu 국수

noon jeong.o 정오

nor ...do ttohan ...anida/-ji anta ...도 또한 ... 아니다/-지 않다

normal jeongsangjeogida, jeongsangjeogin 정상적이다/ -적인

normally botong 보통

north bukjjok 북쪽

north-east bukdongjjok 북동 쪽

north-west bukseojjok 북서 쪽

nose ko 코

nostril kokkumeong 콧구멍

not ...anida/-ji anta ... 아니다/ -지 않다

not only...but also ...ppunman anira ...do ... 뿐만 아니라 ...도

not yet ajik 아직

note (currency) jipye 지폐

note (written) memo 메모

notebook gongchaek 공책

note down, to sseuda, jeokda 쓰다, 적다

nothing amugeotdo anim 아 무것도 아님

notice tongji, yego 통지, 예고

notice, to arachaeda 알아 채다

novel soseol 소설

November sibirwol 십일월

now jigeum 지금

O

nowadays yojeum 요즘
nowhere eodiedo ...eopda 어디에도 ... 없다
nude nache 나체
numb gamgagi eopda/eomneun 감각이 없다/없는
number sujja, beonho 숫자, 번호
nurse ganhosa, yumo 간호사, 유모
nylon naillon 나일론

O

obedient sunjonghada/-haneun 순종하다/-하는
obey, to sunjonghada, ttareuda 순종하다, 따르다
obvious myeongbaekhada, myeongbaekan 명백하다/-한
object, protest, to andaehada 반대하다
object, thing mulche, samul 물체, 사물
occasionally gakkeum 가끔
occupation jigeop 직업
ocean daeyang, bada 대양, 바다
o'clock ...si ...시
October siwol 시월
odor, bad smell naemsae 냄새
of, from ...jung.e, ...eseo ... 중에, ... 에서
of course mullon 물론
off (gone bad) sanghada 상하다
off (turned off) kkeojyeo itda 꺼져 있다
off: to turn something off kkeuda 끄다
offend, to gibun sanghage hada, eogida 기분 상하게 하다, 어기다
offer, suggest, to je.uihada 제의하다

offering (church) heon.geum 헌금
office samusil 사무실
official, formal gongsik(ui) 공식(의)
officials (government) gongmuwon 공무원
often jaju 자주
oil gireum 기름
okay jota, gwaenchanta 좋다, 괜찮다
old (of persons) nai manta/maneun 나이 많다/많은
old (of things) oraedoeda, oraedoen 오래되다, 오래된
olden times, in yennal 옛날
older brother or sister hyeong/nuna, oppa/eonni 형/ 누나, 오빠 etc
on, at ...wie ... 위에
on (of dates) ...e ...에
on (turned on) kyeojyeo itda 켜져 있다
on: to turn something on kyeoda 켜다
on board tago itda 타고 있다
on fire bultago itda 불타고 있다
on foot georeoseo 걸어서
on the way oneun/ganeun gire 오는/ 가는 길에
on the whole daechero 대체로
on time je sigane 제 시간에
once ilttan 일단
one hana 하나
one-way ticket pyeondopyo 편도표
one which, the -(eu)n/neun/(eu)l+(object) -(으)ㄴ / 는 /(으)ㄹ +(사물)
onion yangpa 양파
only danji, ...man 단지, ...만
open yeollida, yeollin 열리다, 열린
open, to yeolda 열다

opinion uigyeon 의견

opponent sangdaebang 상대방

opportunity gihoe 기회

oppose, to bandaehada 반대하다

opposed, in opposition bandae.un 반대의

opposite (contrary) bandae(ui) 반대(의)

opposite (facing) majeun pyeon(ui) 맞은 편(의)

optional seontaekjeogida, seontaekjeogin 선택적이다 / -적인

or ttoneun 또는

orange (color) orenjisaek(ui) 오렌지 색(의)

orange, citrus orenji 오렌지

order (command) myeongnyeong 명령

order (placed for food, goods) jumun 주문

order, command, to myeongnyeonghada 명령하다

order, sequence sunseo 순서

order something, to jumunhada 주문하다

orderly, organized jeongdondoeda / -doen 정돈되다 / -된

ordinary pyeongbeomhada / -han 평범하다 / -한

organize, to maryeonhada, jeongnihada 마련하다, 정리하다

origin chulcheo 출처

original wonbon 원본

originate, come from, to yuraehada 유래하다

ornament jangsik(mul) 장식(물)

orphan goa 고아

other dareun 다른

otherwise geureochi aneumyeon 그렇지 않으면

ought to -a/eoya hada -아/어야 하다

our uri(ui) 우리(의)

out ...bakke ...밖에

outline yoyak 요약

outside bakkat(jjok) 바깥(쪽)

outside of ...ui bakkate ...의 바깥에

oval (shape) tawonhyeong(ui) 타원형(의)

oven obeun 오븐

over, finished kkeunnada 끝나다

over: to turn over dwijipda 뒤집다

overcast, cloudy heurida, heurin 흐리다, 흐린

overcome, to igyeonaeda 이겨내다

overseas hae.oe(ui) 해외(의)

over there jeogi 저기

overturned dwijibeojida, dwijibeojin 뒤집어지다, 뒤집어진

owe, to bitjida 빚지다

own, to soyuhada 소유하다

own, personal jasinui 자신의

own, on one's seuseuro 스스로

oyster gul 굴

P

pack, to ssada 싸다

package jim 짐

page peiji 페이지

paid jibuldoeda, jibuldoen 지불되다, 지불된

pain tongjjeung 통증

painful apeuda, apeun 아프다, 아픈

paint peinteu 페인트

paint (a painting), to geurida 그리다

paint (house, furniture), to chilhada 칠하다

painting geurim, chil 그림, 칠

pair of, a han ssang 한 쌍
pajamas pajama 파자마
palace gung 궁
pan naembi 냄비
panorama panorama 파노라마
panties paenti 팬티
pants baji 바지
paper jong.i 종이
parcel sopo 소포
pardon me? mworago hasyeosseoyo? 뭐라고 하셨어요?
parents bumo 부모
park gong.won 공원
park (car), to juchahada 주차하다
parliament gukhoe 국회
part (not whole) bubun 부분
part (of machine) busok 부속
participate, to chamgahada 참가하다
particularly, especially teukhi 특히
partly bubunjeogeuro 부분적으로
partner (in business) dong.eopja 동업자
partner (spouse) bae.uja 배우자
party (event) pati 파티
party (political) jeongdang 정당
pass (exam), to hapgyeokhada 합격하다
pass, go past, to tonggwahada 통과하다
passenger seunggaek 승객
passion jeongnyeol 정열
passport yeokkwon 여권
password amho 암호
past, former jinada, jinan 지나다, 지난
past: go past, to tonggwahada 통과하다

pastime soilkkeori 소일거리
patient (calm) innaesimitda/- inneun 인내심 있다/- 있는
patient (doctor's) hwanja 환자
pattern, design dijain 디자인
patterned munui(ui) 무늬(의)
pay, to jibulhada 지불하다
pay attention, to jumokhada 주목하다
payment jibul, jiburaek 지불, 지불액
peace pyeonghwa 평화
peaceful pyeonghwaropda, pyeonghwaroun 평화롭다/- 로운
peak, summit jeongsang 정상
peanut ttangkong 땅콩
pearl jinju 진주
peas wandukong 완두콩
peel, to kkeopjireul beotgida 껍질을 벗기다
pen pen 펜
penalty beolgeum 벌금
pencil yeonpil 연필
penis (namja) seonggi (남자) 성기
people saramdeul 사람들
pepper, black huchu 후추
pepper, chilli gochu 고추
percent peosenteu 퍼센트
percentage biyul 비율
perfect wanbyeokhada, wanbyeokan 완벽하다/- 한
performance suhaeng, yeon.gi 수행, 연기
perfume hyangsu 향수
perhaps, maybe ama 아마
period (end of a sentence) machimpyo 마침표
period (menstrual) saengni 생리
period (of time) gigan 기간
permanent yeonggujeogida/- jeogin 영구적이다/-적인
permit, licence heoga 허가

permit, allow, to heorakhada
허락하다
person saram 사람
personality seongkkyeok 성
격
perspire, to ttamheullida 땀
흘리다
pet animal aewandongmul
애완동물
petrol hwiballyu 휘발유
petrol station juyuso 주유소
pharmacy, drugstore yakguk
약국
Philippines pillipin 필리핀
photocopy boksa 복사
photocopy, to boksahada 복
사하다
photograph sajin 사진
photograph, to sajin jjikda
사진 찍다
pick, choose, to
seontaekhada 선택하다
pick up (someone), to
taewojuda 태워주다
pick up, lift (something), to
jupda 줍다
pickpocket somaechigi 소매
치기
pickpocket, to
somaechigihada 소매치기하다
picture geurim 그림
piece, item ...gae ...개
piece, portion, section jogak
조각
pierce, penetrate, to ttulta
뚫다
pig dwaeji 돼지
pillow begae 베개
pills allyak 알약
pineapple painaepeul 파인애
플
pink pingkeusaek(ui) 핑크색
(의)
pitcher tusu 투수
pity: what a pity!
andwaetda! 안 됐다!
place jangso 장소

place, put, to nota 놓다
plain (level ground)
pyeongpyeonghada /-han 평
평하다/-한
plain (not fancy)
dansunhada, dansunhan 단
순하다, 단순한
plan gyehoek 계획
plan, to gyehoekhada 계획하
다
plane bihaenggi 비행기
plant singmul 식물
plant, to simda 심다
plastic peullaseutik 플라스틱
plate jeopsi 접시
play, to nolda,
(gyeonggireul)hada 놀다, (경
기를)하다
play around, to gajigo nolda
가지고 놀다
plead, to tanwonhada 탄원하
다
pleasant gibun jota /jo.eun
기분 좋다/좋은
please (go ahead) geureoke
haseyo 그렇게 하세요
please (request for help)
butakhamnida 부탁합니다
**please (request for
something)** -eo/a juseyo
-어/아 주세요
pleased gippeuda, gippeohada
기쁘다, 기뻐하다
plug (bath) magae 마개
plug (electric) peulleogeu 플
러그
plum jadu 자두
plus peulleoseu 플러스
pocket hojumeoni 호주머니
point (in time) sijjeom 시점
point, dot jeom 점
point out, to jijeokhada 지적
하다
poison dok(yak) 독(약)
poisonous dogi itda /inneun
독이 있다/있는
police gyeongchal 경찰·

police officer

police officer
gyeongchalgwan 경찰관
police station gyeongchalseo
경찰서
polish, to dakda 닦다
politics jeongchihak 정치학
polite gongsonhada,
gongsonhan 공손하다, 공
손한
pollution oyeom 오염
poor gananhada, gananhan
가난하다, 가난한
popular inkki itda/inneun 인
기 있다/있는
population in.gu 인구
pork dwaejigogi 돼지고기
port hanggu 항구
portion, serve ...inbun ...인
분
possess, to soyuhada 소유
하다
possessions soyumul 소유물
possible ganeunghada,
ganeunghan 가능하다, 가
능한
possibly ama 아마
post, column gidung 기둥
post, mail, to buchida 부치
다
postcard yeopseo 엽서
post office ucheguk 우체국
postpone, to yeon.gihada 연
기하다
postponed yeon.gidoeda,
yeon.gidoen 연기되다, 연
기된
pot naembi, hwabun 냄비,
화분
potato gamja 감자
poultry gageum(nyu) 가금
(류)
pour, to butda 붓다
powder garu 가루
power him 힘
powerful himitda, himinneun
힘 있다, 힘 있는
practice yeonseup 연습

practice, to yeonseuphada
연습하다
praise chingchan 칭찬
praise, to chingchanhada 칭
찬하다
prawn sae.u 새우
pray, to gidohada 기도하다
prayer gidomun 기도문
precious gwijunghada,
gwijunghan 귀중하다, 귀
중한
prefer, to seonhohada 선호
하다
pregnant imsinhada, imsinhan
임신하다, 임신한
prepare, make ready, to
junbihada 준비하다
prepared, ready junbidoeda,
junbidoen 준비되다, 준비된
prescription cheobang(jeon)
처방(전)
present (gift) seonmul 선물
present (here) chulseokhada,
chulseokan 출석하다, 출석한
present, to seonmulhada,
jechulhada 선물하다, 제출
하다
present moment, at the
jigeum, hyeonjae 지금, 현재
presently, nowadays yojeum
요즘
president daetongnyeong,
sajang 대통령, 사장
press, journalism eollon 언
론
press, to nureuda 누르다
pressure amnyeok 압력
pretend, to -(eu)n/neun che
hada -(으)ㄴ/는 체 하다
pretty (of things)
areumdapda, areumdaun 아
름답다, 아름다운
pretty (of women) yeppeuda,
yeppeun 예쁘다, 예쁜
pretty, very aju 아주
prevent, to bangjihada 방지
하다

previous ijeon(ui) 이전(의)
price gagyeok 가격
pride jabusim 자부심
priest sinbu 신부
prime minister susang 수상
print, to inswaehada 인쇄
하다
prison gamok 감옥
private sajjeogida, sajjeogin
사적이다, 사적인
prize sang 상
probably ama 아마
problem munje 문제
produce, to saengsanhada
생산하다
profession jigeop 직업
professor gyosu 교수
profit iik 이익
program, schedule
peurogeuraem 프로그램
promise, to yaksokhada 약속
하다
pronounce, to bareumhada
발음하다
proof jeunggeo 증거
property jaesan 재산
protect, to bohohada 보호
하다
protest, to hang.uihada 항의
하다
proud jarangseureopda,
jarangseureon 자랑스럽다/-
스런
prove, to jeungmyeonghada
증명하다
provide, to gonggeuphada
공급하다
public gonggong(ui) 공공(의)
publish, to chulpanhada 출판
하다
pull, to danggida 당기다
pump peompeu 펌프
punctual siganeul jal
jikida /jikineun 시간을 잘 지
키다/지키는
pupil haksaeng, donggong
학생, 동공

pure sunsuhada, sunsuhan
순수하다, 순수한
purple jajusaek(ui) 자주색(의)
purpose mokjeok 목적
purse (for money) jigap
지갑
push, to milda 밀다
put, place, to nota 놓다
put off, delay, to yeon.gihada
연기하다
put on (clothes), to ipda 입
다
puzzled eoridungjeolhada /
-haehada 어리둥절하다/-해
하다
pyjamas pajama 파자마

Q

qualification jagyeok 자격
quarrel maldatum 말다툼
quarter sa bunui il 4분의1
queen yeowang 여왕
question jilmun, munje 질문,
문제
queue, line jul 줄
queue, line up, to julseoda
줄서다
quick ppareuda, ppareun 빠
르다, 빠른
quickly ppalli 빨리
quit, to geumanduda 그만
두다
quiet joyonghada, joyonghan
조용하다, 조용한
quite (fairly) sangdanghi 상
당히
quite (very) aju 아주

R

radio radio 라디오
rail: by rail gicharo 기차로
railroad, railway cheoltto 철
도
rain bi 비
rain, to biga oda 비가 오다
raise, lift, to (deureo)ollida
(들어)올리다

87

raise (children), to

R

raise (children), to
yang.yukhada 양육하다
rank, station in life jiwi 지위
ranking sunwi 순위
rare (scarce) deumulda,
deumun 드물다, 드문
rare (uncooked) seorikda,
seorigeun 설익다, 설익은
rarely, seldom geo.i -ji anta
거의 -지 않다
rat jwi 쥐
rate, tariff yogeum 요금
**rate of exchange (for foreign
currency)** hwannyul 환율
rather, fairly sangdanghi 상
당히
rather than... ...boda ohiryeo
...보다 오히려
raw, uncooked nal (geosui)
날 (것의)
reach, get, to dochakhada 도
착하다
react, to baneunghada 반응
하다
reaction, response baneung
반응
read, to ikda 읽다
ready junbideoda, junbideon
준비되다, 준비된
ready, make, to junbisikida
준비시키다
ready, to get junbihada 준비
하다
real siljje(ui) 실제(의)
realize, be aware of, to
arachaeda 알아채다
really (in fact) siljjero 실제로
really (very) jeongmal 정말
really? jeongmaryo? 정말요?
rear, tail dwi 뒤
reason iyu 이유
reasonable (sensible)
hamnijeogida/-jeogin 합리적
이다/-적인
reasonable (price)
jeokdanghada/-han 적당하다
/-한

receipt yeongsujeung 영수증
receive, to batda 받다
recipe joribeop 조리법
recognize, to araboda 알아
보다
recommend, to
chucheonhada 추천하다
recovered, cured
hoebokhada, hoebokan 회복
하다, 회복한
rectangle jiksagakhyeong 직
사각형
red ppalgata, ppalgan 빨갛다,
빨간
reduce, to ju(ri)da 줄(이)다
reduction chukso 축소
reflect, to bansahada 반사하
다
refrigerator naengjanggo 냉
장고
refusal geojeol 거절
refuse, to geojeolhada 거절
하다
regarding ...e gwanhayeo
...에 관하여
region jiyeok, jibang 지역, 지방
register, to deungnokhada
등록하다
registered post deunggi
upyeon 등기 우편
regret, to huhoehada,
yugamseureupda 후회하다,
유감스럽다
regrettably
yugamseureopgedo 유감스
럽게도
regular, normal botong(ui)
보통(의)
reject, to geojeolhada 거절하
다
relationship gwan.gye 관계
relatives, family chincheok
친척
relax, to ginjang.eul pulda 긴
장을 풀다
release, to pureonota 풀어놓
다

religion jonggyo 종교
remainder, leftover nameoji 나머지
remains (historical) yumul 유물
remember, to gi.eokhada 기억하다
remind, to sanggisikida 상기시키다
rent, to imdaehada 임대하다
rent out, to sejuda 세주다
repair, to gochida 고치다
repeat, to banbokhada 반복하다
replace, to daechehada 대체하다
reply, response, to baneunghada 반응하다
reply (in speech), to daedaphada 대답하다
reply (in writing or deeds), to dapjanghada 답장하다
report bogo 보고
report, to bogohada 보고하다
reporter gija 기자
request (formally), to yocheonghada 요청하다
request (informally), to butakhada 부탁하다
rescue, to gujohada 구조하다
research yeon.gu 연구
research, to yeon.guhada 연구하다
resemble, to damda 닮다
reservation yeyak 예약
reserve (ask for in advance), to yeyakhada 예약하다
reserve (for animals) bohoguyeok 보호구역
resident, inhabitant jumin 주민
resolve (a problem), to haegyeolhada 해결하다
respect jon.gyeong 존경
respect, to jon.gyeonghada 존경하다

respond, react, to baneunghada 반응하다
response, reaction baneung 반응
responsibility chaegim 책임
responsible, to be chaegim itda/inneun 책임 있다/ 있는
rest, remainder nameoji 나머지
rest, relax, to swida 쉬다
restaurant sikdang 식당
restrain, to eokjehada 억제하다
restroom hwajangsil 화장실
result gyeolgwa 결과
resulting from, as a result gyeolgwaroseo 결과로서
retired toejikhada, toejikan 퇴직하다, 퇴직한
return, go back, to doragada, doraoda 돌아가다, 돌아오다
return, give back , to dollyeojuda 돌려주다
return home, to jibe doraoda 집에 돌아오다
return ticket wangbokpyo 왕복표
reveal (make known), to pongnohada 폭로하다
reveal (make visible), to boida 보이다
reverse, back up, to dwiro gada 뒤로 가다
reversed, backwards geokkuro(ui) 거꾸로(의)
ribbon ribon 리본
rice (cooked) bap 밥
rice (plant) byeo 벼
rice (uncooked grains) ssal 쌀
rice fields non 논
rich buyuhada, buyuhan 부유하다, 부유한
rid, get rid of, to jegeohada 제거하다

R

ride, to tada 타다
right, correct olta, oreun 옳다, 옳은
right-hand side oreunjjok 오른쪽
right now jigeum dangjang 지금 당장
rights gwolli 권리
ring (bell), to ullida 울리다
ring (jewellery) banji 반지
ring (on the telephone), to jeonhwahada 전화하다
ripe, to become ikda, igeun 익다, 익은
rise, ascend, to oreuda 오르다
rise, increase, to jeunggahada 증가하다
rival gyeongjaengsangdae 경쟁상대
river gang 강
road doro 도로
roast, grill, to gupda 굽다
roasted, grilled, toasted guun 구운
rock bawi 바위
role yeokhal 역할
roof jibung 지붕
room (in hotel) gaeksil 객실
room (in house) bang 방
room, space gonggan 공간
root (of plant) ppuri 뿌리
rope batjul 밧줄
rotten sseokda, sseogeun 썩다, 썩은
rough geochilda, geochin 거칠다, 거친
roughly, approximately daegang 대강
round (shape) dunggeulda, dunggeun 둥글다, 둥근
round, around ...juwie ...주위에
rubber gomu 고무
rude muryehada, muryehan 무례하다, 무례한
rules gyuchik 규칙
rumor somun 소문

run, to dallida 달리다
run away, to domanggada 도망가다

S

sacred sinseonghada, sinseonghan 신성하다, 신성한
sacrifice hisaeng 희생
sacrifice, to hisaenghada 희생하다
sad seulpeuda, seulpeun 슬프다, 슬픈
safe anjeonhada, anjeonhan 안전하다, 안전한
sail, to hanghaehada 항해하다
salary bonggeup 봉급
sale (reduced prices) seil 세일
sale, for panmae jung 판매 중
sales assistant jeomwon 점원
salt sogeum 소금
salty jjada, jjan 짜다, 짠
same gatda, gateun 같다, 같은
sample gyeonbon 견본
sand morae 모래
sandals saendal 샌달
satisfied manjokhada, manjokaehada 만족하다/-해하다
satisfy, to manjoksikida 만족시키다
Saturday toyoil 토요일
sauce soseu, yangnyeom 소스, 양념
save, keep, to bogwanhada 보관하다
say, to malhada 말하다
say hello, to anbujeonhada 안부전하다
say goodbye, to jal garago jeonhada 잘 가라고 전하다
say sorry, to mianhadago jeonhada 미안하다고 전하다

say thank you, to gomapdago jeonhada 고맙다고 전하다

scales jeo.ul 저울

scarce deumulda, deumun 드물다, 드문

scared museopda, museowohada 무섭다, 무서워하다

scenery gyeongchi 경치

schedule seukejul 스케줄

scholarship janghakgeum 장학금

school hakgyo 학교

schoolchild haksaeng 학생

science gwahak 과학

scissors gawi 가위

score deukjeom 득점

Scotland seukoteullaendeu 스코틀랜드

screen (of computer) seukeurin 스크린

scrub, to munjireuda 문지르다

sculpt, to jogakhada 조각하다

sculpture jogak 조각

sea bada 바다

seafood haemul 해물

seal, to bonghada 봉하다

search for, to chatda 찾다

season gyejeol 계절

seat jari 자리

second du beonjjae 두 번째

secret bimil 비밀

secret, to keep a bimireul jikida 비밀을 지키다

secretary biseo 비서

secure, safe anjeonhada, anjeonhan 안전하다, 안전한

see, to boda 보다

seed ssi 씨

seek, to chatda 찾다

seem, to ...(eu)ro boida ...(으)로 보이다

see you later! tto/najung.e bopsida! 또/나중에 봅시다!

seldom geo.i -ji anta 거의 -지 않다

select, to goreuda 고르다

self jagi 자기

sell, to palda 팔다

send, to bonaeda 보내다

sensible bunbyeollyeok itda/inneun 분별력 있다/있는

sentence munjang, seon.go 문장, 선고

separate gakgak(ui) 각각(의)

separate, to bullihada 분리하다

September guwol 구월

sequence, order sunseo 순서

serious (not funny) simgakhada, simgakan 심각하다, 심각한

serious (severe) jungdaehada, jungdaehan 중대하다, 중대한

servant hain 하인

serve, to mosida 모시다

service seobiseu 서비스

sesame oil chamgireum 참기름

sesame seeds chamkkae 참깨

set seteu 세트

seven ilgop, chil 일곱, 칠

seventeen yeorilgop, sipchil 열일곱, 십칠

seventy ilheun, chilsip 일흔, 칠십

several yeoreo 여러

severe simhada, simhan 심하다, 심한

sew, to baneujilhada 바느질하다

sex, gender seongbyeol 성별

sex, sexual activity sekseu 섹스

shack panjajip 판자집

shade geuneul 그늘

shadow geurimja 그림자

shake, to tteolda 떨다
shake something, to
heundeulda 흔들다
shall, will -(eu)l geosida -(으)
ㄹ 것이다
shallow yatda, yateun 얕다,
얕은
shame, disgrace suchi 수치
shame! what a shame!
changpihada! 창피하다!
shampoo syampu 샴푸
shape moyang 모양
shape, form, to
hyeongseonghada 형성하다
shark sang.eo 상어
sharp nalkaropda, nalkaroun
날카롭다, 날카로운
shave, to myeondohada 면
도하다
she, her geu yeoja 그 여자
(의)
sheep yang 양
sheet (for bed) siteu 시트
sheet (of paper) jang 장
shiny binnada, binnaneun 빛
나다, 빛나는
ship bae 배
shirt syeocheu 셔츠
shit ttong 똥
shiver, to tteolda 떨다
shoes sinbal 신발
shoot, to ssoda 쏘다
shop, store gage 가게
shop, go shopping, to
syopinghada 쇼핑하다
shopkeeper jeomwon 점원
short (concise) gandanhada,
gandanhan 간단하다, 간단한
short (not tall) jakda, jageun
작다, 작은
shorts (short trousers)
banbaji 반바지
shorts (underpants) paenti
팬티
short time, a moment jamsi
잠시
shoulder eokkae 어깨

shout, to oechida 외치다
show (broadcast) syopeuro,
bangsong 쇼프로, 방송
show (live performance) syo
쇼
show, to boyeojuda 보여
주다
shower (for washing) syawo
샤워
shower (of rain) sonagi 소나
기
shower, to take a syawohada
샤워하다
shrimp, prawn sae.u 새우
shut dathida, dachin 닫히다,
닫힌
shut, to datda 닫다
sibling hyeongje 형제
sick, ill apeuda, apeun 아프
다, 아픈
sick, to be (vomit)
meseukkeopda 메스껍다
side jjok 쪽
sightseeing
sinaegwan.gwang 시내관광
sign, symbol pyosi 표시
sign, to sainhada 사인하다
signature seomyeong, sain
서명, 사인
signboard ganpan 간판
silent goyohada, goyohan 고
요하다, 고요한
silk silkeu 실크
silly eoriseokda, eoriseogeun
어리석다, 어리석은
silver eun 은
similar biseuthada, biseutan
비슷하다, 비슷한
simple (easy) swipda, swiun
쉽다, 쉬운
simple (uncomplicated)
gandanhada, gandanhan 간
단하다/-한
since ...[-(eu)n] ihu, -gi
ttaemune ...[-(으)ㄴ] 이후,
-기 때문에
sing, to noraehada 노래하다

Singapore singgapol 싱가폴
single (not married)
doksin(ui) 독신(의)
single (only one) dan hana(ui)
단 하나(의)
sir (term of address)
seonsaengnim 선생님
sister jamae 자매
sister-in-law olke, sinu.i,
hyeongsu 올케, 시누이, 형수
etc
sit (the test), to (siheom)
boda (시험) 보다
sit down, to an(j)da 앉다
situated, to be wichihada 위
치하다
situation, how things are
sanghwang 상황
six yeoseot, yuk 여섯, 육
sixteen yeolyeoseot, simnyuk
열여섯, 십육
sixty yesun, yuksip 예순,
육십
size saijeu 사이즈
skewer kkochaeng.i 꼬챙이
skillful neungsukhada,
neungsukan 능숙하다, 능숙한
skin pibu 피부
skirt chima 치마
sky haneul 하늘
sleep, to jada 자다
sleepy jollida, jollin 졸리다,
졸린
slender ganeudarata,
ganeudaran 가느다랗다, 가
느다란
slight yakganui 약간의
slightly yakgan 약간
slim nalssinhada, nalssinhan
날씬하다, 날씬한
slip (petticoat, underskirt)
seullip 슬립
slippers seullipeo 슬리퍼
slope gyeongsa 경사
slow neurida, neurin 느리다,
느린
slowly cheoncheonhi 천천히

small jakda, jageun 작다,
작은
smart ttokttokhada, ttokttokan
똑똑하다, 똑똑한
smell, bad odor naemsae 냄
새
smell, to naemsaenada,
naemsaematda 냄새나다, 냄
새맡다
smile, to misojitda
미소짓다
smoke yeon.gi 연기
smoke (tobacco), to dambae
pida 담배 피다
smooth (of surfaces)
maekkeureopda/-reo.un 매
끄럽다/-러운
smooth (to go smoothly)
sunjoropda/-roun 순조롭다/-
로운
smuggle, to milsuhada 밀수
하다
snake baem 뱀
sneeze jaechaegi 재채기
sneeze, to jaechaegihada 재
채기하다
snore, to ko golda 코 골다
snow nun 눈
snow, to nuni oda 눈이 오다
so, therefore geuraeseo 그
래서
soak, to jeoksida 적시다
soap binu 비누
soccer chukgu 축구
social sahoe(jeogin) 사회
(적인)
socket (electric) soketeu 소
케트
socks yangmal 양말
sofa, couch sopa 소파
soft budeureopda,
budeureo.un 부드럽다, 부드
러운
soft drink eumnyosu 음료수
sold pallida, pallin 팔리다,
팔린
soldier gunin 군인

S

sold out maejin 매진

sole, only yu.ilhan 유일한

solid dandanhada/-han, goche 단단하다/-한, 고체

solve (a problem), to haegyeolhada 해결하다

some eotteon, yakgan(ui) 어떤, 약간(의)

somebody, someone eotteon saram 어떤 사람

something eotteon geot 어떤 것

sometimes gakkeum 가끔

somewhere eodin.ga 어딘가

son adeul 아들

son-in-law sawi 사위

song norae 노래

soon got 곧

sore, painful apeuda, apeun 아프다, 아픈

sorrow seulpeum 슬픔

sorry, regretful yugamseureopda/-seureo.un 유감스럽다/-스러운

sorry! mianhamnida! 미안합니다!

sort, type jongnyu 종류

sort out, deal with, to cheorihada 처리하다

so that geuraeseo 그래서

sound, noise sori 소리

soup (clear) guk 국

soup (spicy stew) jjigae 찌개

sour sida, sin 시다, 신

source chulcheo 출처

south namjjok 남쪽

south-east namdongjjok 남동쪽

south-west namseojjok 남서쪽

souvenir ginyeompum 기념품

so very aju 아주

soy sauce ganjang 간장

space gonggan 공간

spacious neopda, neolbeun 넓다, 넓은

speak, to malhada 말하다

special teukbyeolhada/-han 특별하다/-한

spectacles an.gyeong 안경

speech yeonseol 연설

speech, to make a yeonseolhada 연설하다

speed sokdo 속도

spell, to cheoljjahada 철자하다

spend, to sseuda, bonaeda 쓰다, 보내다

spices yangnyeom, hyangnyo 양념, 향료

spicy maepda, mae.un 맵다, 매운

spinach sigeumchi 시금치

spine cheokchu 척추

spiral naseonhyeong(ui) 나선형(의)

spirits, hard liquor dokan sul 독한 술

spoiled (does not work) manggajida, manggajin 망가지다/-진

spoiled (of food) sanghada, sanghan 상하다, 상한

spoon sukkarak 숟가락

sponge seupeonji 스펀지

sports seupocheu 스포츠

spotted (pattern) jeommuneu(ui) 점무늬(의)

spray seupeurei 스프레이

spring (metal part) yongsucheol 용수철

spring (of water) oncheon 온천

spring (season) bom 봄

spouse bae.uja 배우자

square (shape) jeongsagakhyeong 정사각형

square, town square gwangjang 광장

squid ojing.eo 오징어

staff jigwon 직원

stain eolluk 얼룩

stairs gyedan 계단

stall (car), to seobeorida 서 버리다
stall (of vendor) panmaedae 판매대
stamp (ink) seutaempeu 스 탬프
stamp (postage) upyo 우표
stand, to seoda 서다
stand up, to ireoseoda 일어 서다
star byeol 별
start, beginning sijak 시작
start, to sijakhada 시작하다
stationery mun.guryu 문구류
statue dongsang 동상
stay, remain, to meomureuda 머무르다
stay overnight, to mukda 묵다
steal, to humchida 훔치다
steam jeunggi 증기
steamed jjida, jjin 찌다, 찐
steel gangcheol 강철
steer, to dollida 돌리다
step dan.gye 단계
steps, stairs gyedan 계단
stick, pole makdaegi 막대기
stick out, to twi.eonaoda 튀어나오다
stick to, to butda 붙다
sticky kkeunjeok.kkeunjeokhada/ -han 끈적끈적하다/-한
sticky rice ilbanmi 일반미
stiff ppeotppeothada/-han 뻣 뻣하다/-한
still, even now ajik 아직
still, quiet goyohada, goyohan 고요하다, 고요한
stink, to naemsaenada 냄새 나다
stomach, belly bae 배
stone dol 돌
stool geolsang 걸상
stop (bus, train) jeongnyujang 정류장
stop, halt, to meomchuda 멈추다

stop, cease, to geumanduda 그만두다
stop by, pay a visit, to deulleuda 들르다
stop it! geumanduseyo! 그 만두세요!
store, shop gage 가게
store, to jeojanghada 저장하 다
storey (of a building) ...cheung jjari ...층 짜리
storm pokpung 폭풍
story (tale) iyagi 이야기
stout ttungttunghada/-han 뚱뚱하다/-한
stove, cooker seutobeu 스토 브
straight ttokbareuda, ttokbareun 똑바르다, 똑바른
straight ahead ttokbaro 똑바 로
strait haehyeop 해협
strange isanghada, isanghan 이상하다, 이상한
stranger natseon saram 낯 선 사람
street geori 거리
strength him 힘
strict eomgyeokhada, eomgyeokan 엄격하다/- 한
strike, to go on pa.eophada 파업하다
strike, hit, to chida, ttaerida 치다, 때리다
string kkeun 끈
striped julmunui(ui) 줄무늬 (의)
strong himseda, himsen 힘 세다, 힘 센
stubborn, determined gojip seda/sen 고집 세다/ 센
stuck, won't move umjigiji anta/anneun 움직이지 않다 /않 는
student haksaeng 학생
study, learn, to gongbuhada 공부하다

stupid eoriseokda, eoriseogeun 어리석다, 어리석은

style seutail 스타일

succeed, to seonggonghada 성공하다

success seonggong 성공

such geureon 그런

such as, for example yereul deuljamyeon 예를 들자면

suck, to ppalda 빨다

suddenly gapjagi 갑자기

suffer, to gyeokda 겪다

suffering gotong 고통

sugar seoltang 설탕

sugarcane satangsusu 사탕수수

suggest, to je.anhada 제안하다

suggestion je.an 제안

suit, business jeongjang 정장

suitable, fitting jeokdanghada, jeokdanghan 적당하다/-한

suitcase yeohaenggabang 여행가방

summer yeoreum 여름

summit, peak jeongsang 정상

sun taeyang 태양

Sunday iryoil 일요일

sunlight haeppit 햇빛

sunny hwachanghada/-han 화창하다/-한

sunrise ilchul 일출

sunset ilmol 일몰

supermarket supeomaket 수퍼마켓

suppose, to gajeonghada 가정하다

sure hwaksilhada, hwaksilhan 확실하다, 확실한

surf pado 파도

surface pyomyeon 표면

surface mail bihanggong.upyeon 비항공우편

surname seong 성

surprised nollada, nollawohada 놀라다, 놀라워하다

surprising nollapda, nollaun 놀랍다, 놀라운

surroundings juwibaegyeong 주위배경

survive, to saranamda 살아남다

suspect, to uisimhada 의심하다

suspicion hyeomui 혐의

swallow, to samkida 삼키다

sweat ttam 땀

sweat, to ttam heullida 땀흘리다

sweep, to sseulda 쓸다

sweet dalda, dan 달다, 단

sweet, dessert dijeoteu 디저트

sweet and sour saekomdalkomhada/han 새콤달콤하다/ 한

sweet corn .oksusu 옥수수

sweets, candy satang 사탕

swim, to suyeonghada 수영하다

swimming costume, swimsuit suyeongbok 수영복

swimming pool suyeongjang 수영장

swing, to heundeulda 흔들다

switch seuwichi 스위치

switch, change, to bakkuda 바꾸다

switch on, turn on, to kyeoda 켜다

synthetic hapseong(ui) 합성(의)

T

table teibeul 테이블

tablecloth teibeul ppo 테이블 보

tablemat jeopsibatchim 접시받침

tablets allyak 알약

tail kkori 꼬리

take, remove, to gajyeogada 가져가다

take care of, to dolboda 돌보다

take off (clothes), to beotda 벗다

talk, to malhada 말하다

talk about, to ...e daehae malhada ...에 대해 말하다

tall ki keuda/keun 키 크다/큰

tame gildeuryeojida/-yeojin 길들여지다/-여진

Taoism dogyo 도교

tape, adhesive teipeu 테이프

tape recording nogeum 녹음

taste mat 맛

taste (sample), to matboda 맛보다

taste (salty, spicy), to masi nada 맛이 나다

tasty masitda, masinneun 맛있다, 맛있는

taxi taeksi 택시

tea cha 차

teach, to gareuchida 가르치다

teacher seonsaengnim 선생님

team tim 팀

tear, rip, to jjitda 찢다

tears nunmul 눈물

teenager sipdae 십대

teeshirt tisyeocheu 티셔츠

teeth i 이

telephone jeonhwa(gi) 전화(기)

telephone number jeonhwabeonho 전화번호

television tellebijeon 텔레비전

tell (a story), to malhada 말하다

tell (let know), to allida 알리다

temperature ondo 온도

temple jeol, sachal 절, 사찰

temporary imsi(ui) 임시(의)

ten yeol, sip 열, 십

tendon himjjul 힘줄

tennis teniseu 테니스

tens of, multiples of ten susibui 수십의

tense ginjanghada, ginjanghan 긴장하다, 긴장한

ten thousand man 만

terrible museopda, museo.un 무섭다, 무서운

test siheom 시험

test, to teseuteuhada, geomsahada 테스트하다, 검사하다

testicles gohwan 고환

than ...boda ...보다

Thailand taeguk 태국

thank, to gamsahada 감사하다

thank you! gamsahamnida! 감사합니다!

that jeo, jeogeot (object), jeo bun/ae (person) 저, 저것, 저분/애

that (introducing a quotation) ...go hada ...고 하다

that, the one -(eu)n/neun/(eu)l+(person) -(으)ㄴ/는/(으)ㄹ+(사람)

theater (drama) geukjang 극장

their, theirs geudeurui, geudeurui geot 그들의, 그들의 것

then geuttae, geureomyeon 그때, 그러면

there geogi 거기

therefore geureomeuro 그러므로

there is, there are itda 있다

these i, igeotdeul, i bundeul/aedeul 이, 이것들, 이분들/애들

they, them geudeul 그들

T

thick (of liquids) jinhada, jinhan 진하다, 진한

thick (of things) dukkeopda, dukkeo.un 두껍다, 두꺼운

thief doduk 도둑

thigh heobeokji 허벅지

thin (of liquids) mukda, mulgeun 묽다, 묽은

thin (of persons) mareuda, mareun 마르다, 마른

thing mulgeon 물건

think, have an opinion, to saenggakhada 생각하다

think, ponder, to sukgohada 숙고하다

third se beonjjae 세 번째

thirsty mongmareuda, mongmareun 목마르다, 목 마른

thirteen yeolset, sipsam 열 셋, 십삼

thirty seoreun, samsip 서른, 삼십

this i, igeot (object), i bun/ae (person) 이, 이것, 이 분/ 애

those jeo, jeogeotdeul, jeo bundeul/aedeul 저, 저것들, 저 분/ 애들

though birok -jiman/-(eu)l jirado 비록 -지만/-(으)ㄹ 지 라도

thoughts saenggak 생각

thousand cheon 천

thread sil 실

threaten, to wihyeophada 위 협하다

three set, sam 셋, 삼

throat mok(gumeong) 목(구 멍)

through, past ...eul/reul tonghayeo ...을/ 를 통하여

throw, to deonjida 던지다

throw away, throw out, to beorida 버리다

thunder cheondung 천둥

Thursday mogyoil 목요일

thus, so geuraeseo 그래서

ticket (for entertainment) ipjangkkwon 입장권

ticket (for transport) pyo 표

tidy danjeonghada, danjeonghan 단정하다, 단 정한

tidy up, to jeongdonhada 정 돈하다

tie, necktie nektai 넥타이

tie, to maeda 매다

tiger horang.i 호랑이

tight binteumeopda/- eomneun 빈틈없다/- 없 는

time sigan 시간

time, from time to time gakkeum 가끔

times (multiplying) ...bae ... 배

timetable siganpyo 시간표

tiny jakda, jageun 작다, 작은

tip (end) kkeut 끝

tip (gratuity) tip 팁

tired (sleepy) jollida, jollin 졸 리다, 졸린

tired (worn out) pigonhada, pigonhan 피곤하다, 피곤한

title (of book, film) jemok 제 목

title (of person) chingho 칭호

to, toward (a person) ...ege ... 에게

to, toward (a place) ...e, ...(ui)ro ...에, ...(으)로

today oneul 오늘

toe balkkarak 발가락

tofu dubu 두부

together hamkke 함께

toilet hwajangsil 화장실

tomato tomato 토마토

tomorrow nae.il 내일

tongue hyeo 혀

tonight oneulppam 오늘밤

too (also) ttohan 또한

too (excessive) neomu 너무

too much neomu mani 너무 많이

tool, utensil, instrument
dogu 도구
tooth i 이
toothbrush chissol 칫솔
toothpaste chiyak 치약
top kkokdaegi 꼭대기
topic juje 주제
torch, flashlight
sonjeondeung 손전등
total hapgye 합계
touch, to manjida 만지다
tourist gwan.gwanggaek 관
광객
toward, to (direction)
...(eu)ro ...(으)로
towel sugeon 수건
tower tap 탑
town ma.eul, si 마을, 시
toy jangnankkam 장난감
trade, business bijeuniseu,
muyeok 비즈니스, 무역
trade, exchange, to
georaehada 거래하다
traditional jeontongjeok(in)
전통적(인)
traffic gyotong 교통
train gicha 기차
train station yeok 역
training hullyeon 훈련
translate, to beonyeokhada
번역하다
travel, to yeohaenghada 여
행하다
traveler yeohaengja 여행자
tray jaengban 쟁반
treat (behave towards), to
dae.uhada 대우하다
treat (medically), to
chiryohada 치료하다
treat (something special), to
daejeophada 대접하다
tree namu 나무
triangle samgakhyeong 삼각
형
tribe bujok 부족
trip, journey yeohaeng 여행
troops gundae 군대

trouble munje 문제
troublesome golchi
apeuda/apeun 골치 아프다/
아픈
trousers baji 바지
truck teureok 트럭
true sasil ida, sasil(ui) 사실이
다, 사실(의)
truly jeongmallo 정말로
trust, to mitda 믿다
try, to haeboda 해보다
try on (clothes), to ibeo boda
입어 보다
Tuesday hwayoil 화요일
turn (make a turn) charye 차례
turn around, to dolda 돌다
turn off, to kkeuda 끄다
turn on, to kyeoda 켜다
turtle (land) geobuk 거북
turtle (sea) badageobuk 바다
거북
TV tibi 티비
twelve yeolttul, sibi 열둘,
십이
twenty seumul, isip 스물,
이십
two dul, i 둘, 이
type, sort jongnyu 종류
type, to taipinghada 타이핑
하다
typhoon taepung 태풍
typical jeonhyeongjeogida/-
jeogin 전형적이다/-적인

U

ugly motsaenggida,
motsaenggin 못생기다, 못생
긴
umbrella usan 우산
uncle ajeossi 아저씨
uncooked nal (geosui) 날(것
의)
under ...arae ...아래
undergo, to gyeokda 겪다
underpants paenti 팬티
undershirt meriyaseu 메리
야스

understand, to ihaehada 이
해하다
underwear sogot 속옷
undressed, to get ot beotda
옷 벗다
unemployed siljikhada, siljikan
실직하다, 실직한
unfortunately
bulhaenghagedo 불행하게도
unhappy bulhaenghada,
bulhaenghan 불행하다, 불
행한
United Kingdom
daeyeongjeguk 대영제국
United States miguk 미국
university daehak 대학
unless -ji aneumyeon -지 않
으면
unlucky uni eopda/eomneun
운이 없다/ 없는
unnecessary bulpiryohada,
bulpiryohan 불필요하다, 불
필요한
unripe an ikda/igeun 안 익
다/익은
until ...kkaji, -(eu)l ttaekkaji ...
까지, -(으)ㄹ 때까지
up, upward ...wie, ...wiro ...
위에, ... 위로
upset, unhappy gibuni
sanghada/sanghan 기분이
상하다/상한
upside down dwijibeojida,
dwijibeojin 뒤집어지다, 뒤집
어진
upstairs wicheung 위층
urban dosi(ui) 도시(의)
urge, push for, to
jaechokhada 재촉하다
urgent gin.geuphada,
gin.geupan 긴급하다, 긴급한
urinate, to sobyeonboda 소
변보다
use, to sayonghada 사용하다
used to, accustomed -
neunde iksukhada -는데 익
숙하다

used to do something -
gonhaetda -곤 했다
useful sseulmo itda/inneun
쓸모 있다/ 있는
useless sseulmo
eopda/eomneun 쓸모 없다/
없는
usual botong(ui) 보통(의)
usually botong 보통
uterus jagung 자궁

V

vacation (holiday) hyuga 휴
가
vacation (school) banghak
방학
vaccination yebang jeopjong
예방 접종
vagina (yeoja) seonggi (여자)
성기
vague mohohada, mohohan
모호하다, 모호한
valid yuhyohada, yuhyohan
유효하다, 유효한
valley gyegok 계곡
value (cost) gagyeok 가격
value, good gachi 가치
value, to gwihage yeogida
귀하게 여기다
vase kkotbyeong 꽃병
VCR bidio (rekodeu) 비디오
(레코드)
vegetable singmul 식물
vegetables yachae 야채
vehicle charyang 차량
very, extremely aju 아주
vest, undershirt jokki 조끼
via ...eul/reul geochyeoseo
...을/를 거쳐서
video cassette bidio (teipeu)
비디오 (테이프)
video recorder bidio
(rekodeu) 비디오 (레코드)
videotape, to nokhwahada
녹화하다
Vietnam beteunam 베트남
view, look at, to boda 보다

W

view, panorama gyeongchi 경치

village ma.eul 마을

vinegar sikcho 식초

visa bija 비자

visit bangmun 방문

visit, to pay a bangmunhada 방문하다

voice moksori 목소리

voice mail eumseong mesiji 음성 메시지

volcano hwasan 화산

vomit, to tohada 토하다

vote, to tupyohada 투표하다

W

wages jugeup 주급

wait for, to gidarida 기다리다

waiter, waitress jong.eobwon 종업원

wake someone up, to kkae.uda 깨우다

wake up, to kkae.eonada 깨어나다

walk, to geotda 걷다

walking distance gakkaun geori 가까운 거리

wall byeok 벽

wallet jigap 지갑

want, to wonhada 원하다

war jeonjaeng 전쟁

war, to make jeonjaenghada 전쟁하다

warm ttatteuthada, ttatteutan 따뜻하다, 따뜻한

warmth ttatteutam 따뜻함

warn, to gyeonggohada 경고하다

warning gyeonggo 경고

wash, to ssitda 씻다

wash the dishes, to seolgeojihada 설거지하다

watch (show, movie), to boda 보다

watch (wristwatch) (sonmok)sigye (손목)시계

watch, look, see, to boda 보다

watch over, guard, to gyeonghohada 경호하다

water mul 물

water buffalo mulso 물소

waterfall pokpo 폭포

watermelon subak 수박

wave (in sea) pado 파도

wave, to heundeulda, mulgyeolchida 흔들다, 물결치다

wax wakseu 왁스

way, method bangbeop 방법

way, by way of ...eul/reul tonghayeo ...을/를 통해서

way in ipgu 입구

way out chulgu 출구

we, us uri 우리

weak yakhada, yakan 약하다, 약한

wealthy buyuhada, buyuhan 부유하다, 부유한

weapon mugi 무기

wear, to ipda 입다

weary pirohada, pirohan 피로하다, 피로한

weather nalssi 날씨

weave, to (jingmureul) jjada (직물을) 짜다

weaving jjagi 짜기

website wepsaiteu 웹사이트

wedding gyeolhonsik 결혼식

Wednesday suyoil 수요일

week ju 주

weekend jumal 주말

weekly jugan 주간

weep, to ulda 울다

weigh, to mugereul dalda 무게를 달다

weigh out, to daranaeda, gyeonjuda 달아내다, 견주다

weight chejung, muge 체중, 무게

weight, gain, to chejung.i neulda 체중이 늘다

weight, lose, to chejung.i julda 체중이 줄다

welcome! eoseo oseyo! 어서 오세요!

welcome, to hwanyeonghada 환영하다

well (for water) umul 우물

well, good jal 잘

well-behaved pumhaeng.i jota/jo.eun 품행이 좋다/좋은

well-cooked, well-done jal ikda/igeun 잘 익다/익은

well done! jal haesseoyo! 잘 했어요!

well-mannered ye.ibareuda, ye.ibareun 예의바르다/-바른

well off, wealthy buyuhada, buyuhan 부유하다, 부유한

west seojjok 서쪽

westerner seoyang saram 서양 사람

wet jeotda, jeojeun 젖다, 젖은

what? mworagoyo? 뭐라고요?

what for? mwo hasigeyo? 뭐 하시게요?

what kind of? eotteon geoyo? 어떤 거요?

what time? myeot siyo? 몇 시요?

wheel bakwi 바퀴

when? eonjeyo? 언제요?

when, at the time -(eu)l ttae -(으)ㄹ 때

whenever -(eu)l ttaemada -(으)ㄹ 때마다

where? eodiyo? 어디요?

where to? eodiro gaseyo? 어디로 가세요?

which? eoneu geoyo? 어느 거요?

while -neun dong.an -는 동안

white hayata, hayan 하얗다, 하얀

who? nuguyo? 누구요?

whole, all of jeonche(ui) 전체(의)

whole, to be complete wanjeonhada/-han 완전하다, 완전한

why? waeyo? 왜요?

wicked saakhada, saakan 사악하다, 사악한

wide neopda, neolbeun 넓다, 넓은

width pok 폭

widow gwabu 과부

widowed honjadoeda, honjadoen 혼자되다, 혼자된

widower horabi 홀아비

wife anae 아내

wild yasaeng(ui) 야생(의)

will, shall -(eu)l geosida -(으)ㄹ 것이다

win, to igida 이기다

wind, breeze baram 바람

window (for paying, buying tickets) changgu 창구

window (in house) changmun 창문

wine podoju 포도주

wing nalgae 날개

winner useungja 우승자

winter gyeo.ul 겨울

wipe, to dakda 닦다

wire cheolssa 철사

wise hyeonmyeonghada/-han 현명하다/-한

wish, to barada 바라다

with ...hago, ...(eu)ro ...하고, ...(으)로

within reason hapdanghan seoneseo 합당한 선에서

without ...eopsi ...없이

witness mokgyeokja 목격자

witness, to mokgyeokhada 목격하다

woman yeoja 여자

wonderful meotjida, meotjin 멋지다, 멋진

wood namu 나무

wooden namuro doen 나무
로 된
wool ul, yangmo 울, 양모
word daneo 단어
work, occupation il, jigeop
일, 직업
work, to ilhada 일하다
work, function, to
jakdonghada 작동하다
world se.gye 세계
worn out (clothes)
darabeorida, darabeorin 닳아
버리다/-버린
worn out, tired pigonhada,
pigonhan 피곤하다, 피곤한
worry, to geokjeonghada 걱
정하다
worse deo nappeuda/nappeun
더 나쁘다/ 나쁜
worship, to sungbaehada 숭
배하다
worst gajang
nappeuda/nappeun 가장 나
쁘다/나쁜
worth, to be gachi itda 가치
있다
wound sangcheo 상처
wrap, to ssada 싸다
wrist sonmok 손목
write, to sseuda 쓰다
writer jakga 작가
wrong (false) geojisida,
geojit(ui) 거짓이다, 거짓(의)
wrong (mistaken) teullida,
teullin 틀리다, 틀린
wrong (morally) nappeuda,
nappeun 나쁘다, 나쁜

Y

yawn hapum 하품
year yeon 년
years old ...sal, ...se
...살, ...세
yell, to oechida 외치다
yellow norata, noran 노랗다,
노란
yes ne, ye 네, 예
yesterday eoje 어제
yet, not yet ajik 아직
you (audience) yeoreobun
여러분
you (familiar) neo,
neohui(deul) 너, 너희(들)
you (female) agassi, ajumeoni
아가씨, 아주머니
you (male) ajeossi,
seonsaengnim 아저씨,
선생님
you're welcome!
gwaenchanayo! 괜찮아요!,
anieyo 아니에요
young eorida, eorin 어리다,
어린
younger brother or sister
dongsaeng 동생
youth (state of being young)
jeolmeum 젊음
youth (young person)
jeolmeuni 젊은이

Z

zero yeong, gong 영, 공
zoo dongmurwon 동물원
zucchini, courgettes
(ae)hobak (애)호박

ENGLISH—KOREAN